Praise for *Learning to Leave*

Learning to Leave encapsulates the true spirit of my own learning journey - embracing the power of learning by doing. Washor and Boldt challenge and inspire us to break free from conventional classrooms and pursue authentic, transformative learning experiences. A must-read for the bold and the curious who are looking for practical insights on how we may RETHINK education.

Marc Eckō
Founder - Eckō Unltd. and Complex Networks and Chief Creative Officer - XQ Institute

Learning to Leave: How Real-World Learning Transforms Education challenges us to dig deeper into what transformational learning looks like when freed from the chains of old ways, old forms, and old measures. Thought-provoking and edge-exploring, the authors show us what's needed for young people to thrive, and how we bring those approaches to life right now. With numerous stories and examples of students engaging in deep and meaningful learning - IN and WITH community - the authors make it abundantly clear that the only way forward is a rock solid commitment to centering learners and engaging them in things they care about. A must read for anyone interested in making any real change for learners - up close or at a systems level.

Elyse Burden
Executive Director/Co-founder - Real World Scholars

Expanding participation in work-based, real-world learning is the most impactful change we could make to American secondary education because it builds agency, purpose and skills. Ten years after writing the most important book on the topic, Leaving to Learn, Elliot Washor (with Scott Boldt) is back with a new version, *Learning to Leave*, that makes the case for Real-World Learning. With help from American Student Assistance, this book might be the spark that changes the way we think about high school.

Tom Vander Ark
CEO - Getting Smart

"New forms - not re-forms." Amen, Elliot Washor and Scott Boldt. Drawing powerfully from the life-changing inventions of Big Picture Learning, *Learning to Leave* will surely deepen understanding of how learner-centered, real-world learning fuels identity development, leadership, and builds community. It colorfully illustrates what's needed and what's possible if we reimagine education systems.

Kelly Young
President and Founder - Education Reimagined

Learning to Leave offers an emphatic clarion call to policymakers, educators, and parents to leave behind a standardized, obsolete education model and embrace authentic purposeful real-world learning. Drawing on a mosaic of exemplars, the authors inform and inspire us as they bring to life the education principles that develop each child's distinctive potential.

Ted Dintersmith
Founder - What School Could Be

Elliot Washor and Scott Boldt share the compelling lessons that have emerged from the work of Big Picture Learning. BPL's diverse programs provide compelling evidence about the power of real-world learning to prepare young people for the world they will enter once they leave their formal education and, more importantly, invite them to build the sense of purpose and agency we know each person needs to thrive. They point out, however, that real-world learning will never become accessible for all young people until we reconsider the purpose, practice and assessment of learning. Washor and Boldt lay out the New Ways, New Forms and New Measures that all of us - students, parents, educators, policy leaders, funders and community members - need to embrace in order to transform our educational system into one that truly enables us to meet the unique needs and interests of each young person. Filled with anecdotes and real world examples, this book captures the lessons of an inspiring and powerful global network of young people, educators and communities committed to transforming education.

Dr. Ulcca Joshi Hansen
Author of the award-winning book *The Future of Smart: How Our Education System Needs to Change to Help All Young People Thrive*

In essence this book describes why humans learn, and the ways we learn best. No more than 200 years old, the common school movement is perhaps a failed brief experiment in the timeline of humanity. Maybe we need to be learning, connecting and teaching out of the classroom, as has been done for millennia? It's a simple idea, but simple doesn't mean easy. Boiling education down to this core makes it harder to hide unsuccessful results - something unattractive to the educational system. I've been following Elliot Washor's work since the 1990s and borrowing liberally. I learn something every time I read his work or talk with him. Take advantage of the distilled knowledge within this book and see if you have the guts to follow it.

Joe Youcha
Director - Building To Teach

The heart of this book is not about reform but revolution. It sets out to overturn 150 years of a calcified factory model of education that positions young people as a homogenized group of information receptacles. The good news is that the principles articulated by Elliot Washor and Scott Boldt are grounded in millennia of knowledge, in long recognized, tried and true understandings of community-based interactions and embodied experiences.

This work is not for the faint of heart. When the transformations developed in this book are fully understood and implemented, they will bring about new structures of education, that embody our best hopes and aspirations

David Gersten
Distinguished Professor and Director of Interdisciplinary Learning -
The Cooper Union and Founder and President - Arts Letters and Numbers

In *Learning to Leave: How Real-World Learning Transforms Education*, Elliot and Scott invite us to reflect on fundamental questions on the purpose and design of education in the 21st Century. All the pieces of the journey towards transforming education to prepare every child, growing up in any part of the world, fall in place. The book uses evidence to propose credible strategies of addressing the disconnect between schooling and the world of work.

Educators who grapple with the triad questions of how curriculum, learning and assessment can be effectively and efficiently aligned will also find this book extremely useful.

Dr. David Njeng'ere
CEO - Kenya National Examinations Council

Education is in need of a revolution and *Learning to Leave* shows us the way forward. Grounded in solid pedagogical principles, building on successful worldwide practices, and sharing an ethos of deep transformation, this book will change the way you look at schools, teachers, and real-world learners. Washor and Boldt's writing is accessible, insightful, and leaves readers with a rare sense of hope for the future of education.

Vlad Glaveanu
Professor of Psychology - Dublin City University and Adjunct Professor - Centre for the Science of Learning and Technology, University of Bergen and President - Possibility Studies Network

Thanks for the opportunity to review this fantastic book! Even though *Learning to Leave* is about education in the USA, it has great relevance for the UK, especially in the current climate. The focus is on re-engaging young people with meaningful real-world experiences to inspire their future aspirations; it especially prioritizes young people from more vulnerable communities.

The breadth and depth of "New Ways, New Forms, and New Measures" is a testament to the authors leading the way into prioritizing students' interests, relationships and practice and their search for meaning and sense-making in the world. The International Big Picture Learning Credential is a thorough new measure and methodology for engaging young people in student-driven learning plans that enhance key skills of communication, enthusiasm and attitude, teamwork, networking, problem solving, critical thinking and professionalism.

Every young person, regardless of circumstance, should be able to pursue a creative pathway towards a more hopeful future. This book has the potential to inform system change in schools and the wider education systems internationally.

Dr. Penny Hay
Research Fellow - Centre for Cultural and Creative Industries, School of Education, Bath Spa University and Director of Research - House of Imagination, UK

LEARNING to LEAVE

HOW **REAL-WORLD LEARNING** TRANSFORMS EDUCATION

ELLIOT WASHOR • SCOTT BOLDT

BIG
PICTURE
LEARNING

Big Picture Learning
325 Public Street,
Providence, RI 02905
www.bigpicture.org

The authors and publisher wish to thank Digital Products International (DPI), Inc. for permission to use the 1974 Memorex image on page 75.

Library of Congress Cataloging-in-Publication Data
Washor, Elliot and Boldt, Scott.
    Learning to Leave : How Real-World Learning Transforms Education / Elliot Washor and Scott Boldt ; foreword by Jean Eddy - 1st ed.
        pages   cm   (Big Picture Learning)
    Includes bibliographical references.
    ISBN — 979-8-88955-613-8 (acid-free paper)
    1. Educational change-United States.   2. Educational policy-United States.
3. School improvement programs.   4. School management and organization.   5. Educational assessment.   I. Washor, Elliot   II. Boldt, Scott   III. Title

LCCN: 2023905096

Book Design & Concept: Ian Robinson

Printed in the United Kingdom by W&G Baird Ltd.

Elliot

To those who flew
too close to the sun.

Scott

To my Dad - Bob Boldt - whose family
circumstances compelled him to leave to learn
when he was 15 - it wasn't easy, but you did well.

---

*Even if the last move did not
succeed, the inner command
says move again.*

Seamus Heaney

Abbreviations

ACLM   American College of Lifestyle Medicine

AP   Advanced Placement

ARC   Assessment Research Center (University of Melbourne)

ASA   American Student Assistance

BPL   Big Picture Learning

CTE   Career and Technical Education

EASRCC   Eastern Atlantic Regional Council of Carpenters

ELO   Extended Learning Opportunities

ESSA   Every Student Succeeds Act

GED   General Equivalency Diploma (equivalent to a high school diploma)

HFFI   Harbor Freight Fellows Initiative

HVAC   Heating, Ventilation and Air Conditioning

K-12   Kindergarten to 12th Grade

LALtL   Los Angeles Leaves to Learn

LTL   *Leaving to Learn*

L2L   *Learning to Leave*

Perkins V   Strengthening Career and Technical Education for the 21st Century Act

PD   Professional Development

RUBY   The *rubric* designed by ARC for evidence-based competency assessment

RWL   Real-World Learning

TWSBA   Teaching With Small Boats Alliance

WIOA   Workforce Innovation and Opportunity Act

Contents

Foreword   01
Preface   07
Acknowledgements   10
Introduction   11

1. Looking Back   23
Expectations   25
WITH and WANT   27
New Ways, New Forms, New Measures   28
Leading the Way   30

2. New Ways   33
Learning or Teaching   34
Interests-Relationships-Practice   35
Off-track Learning   38
Tacit Knowledge   40
Edge to Center   42
Muddling Through- Mingling With- Mattering To   44
The Game Not the Score   46

3. New Forms   49
Do and Be Able to Know   50
New Forms Not RE-forms   51
B-Unbound   53
Searching for Meaning   55

Harbor Freight Fellows Initiative (HFFI)   58
Project InSight   63
Los Angeles Leaves to Learn (LALtL)   67

4. New Measures   **73**

BPLiving   75
Lifestyle Medicine Measures   76
The International Big Picture Learning Credential (IBPLC) 79
Person-Referenced   81
Learning Frames-Portfolio-Video   82
CTE   86
311 Credential   90

5. Looking Ahead   **97**

American Student Assistance (ASA)   99
Community Response   112
From Interventions to Preventions   113
What Will Change Schools?   116
Learning Plans   119

Bibliography   123

Foreword

by Jean Eddy, *President and CEO of American Student Assistance® (ASA)*

I first read **Leaving to Learn** 10 years ago and immediately knew it would disrupt and influence how we think about getting kids ready for the elusive "what comes next?" Washor and Mojkowski shared their bold strategy for breathing new life into high schools and for getting young people invested in their future and the future of work.

The recipe was simple: reimagine the classroom model to effectively engage young people - particularly those from vulnerable populations - with meaningful work-based and real-world learning experiences that prepare them for postsecondary education and career success.

However, despite the progress made by Big Picture Learning and other visionaries, sadly, many of our kids today are still inadequately prepared to make informed, confident decisions about what they want to do after high school. In the last decade, the world has been transformed in ways we never could have imagined, with the last three years serving as an accelerant of socioeconomic turbulence and a marked equity gap that continues to hurt the most vulnerable kids within our systems. That includes the pandemic-driven growth in the number of 16-24-year-olds who are neither in school nor employed.

Moreover, we know from our own research that only 47 percent of respondents who identified as members of Generation Z said they had enough information to decide what pathway was best for them after high school[1]. At the same time, more and more young people are increasingly skeptical of the high school-to-college route and want more flexible postsecondary education pathways. In the spring of 2022, there were 662,000 fewer students enrolled in undergraduate programs compared to the previous year, and a recent study found that just 53 percent of today's high schoolers say they are likely to attend college[2]. With so many kids uncertain about their futures, doing a better job of getting every kid on the right path based on their interests isn't just a feel-good exercise - it's a necessity.

To this end, helping every kid make informed, confident choices to achieve long-term success after high school is at the forefront of my consciousness and in the minds of my colleagues at American Student Assistance® (ASA). We found that one of the most effective ways to fulfill our mission is by connecting kids with opportunities to explore career possibilities beyond the classroom. This is beautifully articulated in the new book Elliot has written with Scott Boldt, *Learning to Leave: How Real World Learning Transforms Education*. Kids need opportunities to experiment with careers and "test and try" their interests through real-world experiences while they're in middle and high school, so they can better craft a deliberate postsecondary plan based on passions and ultimate career goals.

In tandem with years of advocacy work in this space, we've partnered with and funded many of the country's most forward-thinking organizations and school districts to expand experiential and work-based learning. We've conducted extensive research into models of promise and best practices for work-based learning that every state can learn from - things like agreeing on common guidelines around work-based learning opportunities, developing explicit programming to ensure diverse employer participation, and ensuring adequate funding for all parties involved.

Why work-based learning, though? Work-based learning, it's known, builds six of the most important soft skill areas: communication, enthusiasm and attitude, teamwork, networking, problem solving and critical thinking, and professionalism, yielding for kids a natural edge in achieving career goals and the chance to make professional connections. It is shown to help people carve a pathway into the labor market while positively impacting engagement and retention[3].

We see the power of this model in action through our partnership with Big Picture Learning (BPL), to scale its Learning Through Interests and Internships (LTI) program. Through this program, students have access to informational interviews, shadow days, internships, and mentorships that are integrated within their educational experience. LTI was implemented to accelerate the rate of internships in 150 locations around the nation, while providing professional development for 450 educators and access to BPL's ImBlaze internship management platform.

As a result, the program has reached more than 30,000 high school students, letting them build valuable social capital while boosting their self-confidence and awareness of the working world. Robert Fung, the principal at the San Diego Met High School - one of the program's beneficiaries - shared that, "We have witnessed how Big Picture Learning and [the program] empowers students to take ownership of their search for internships. This agency and motivation breeds confidence and resilience[4]."

Now, BPL is set to develop and grow the organization's outside-of-school, direct-to-learner programs through the B-Unbound platform. This program gives kids real-world learning experiences while empowering them to build skills as they connect the dots between learning and life.

We know from our work over the years in the classroom and out that reaching youth directly is the best way to scale access to these invaluable opportunities across various industries. Doing so prepares young people to enter a workforce where hiring managers are looking beyond the degree for signifiers of people's readiness for good paying jobs. That is to say that skills-based hiring isn't a future-state, it's already on the rise.

Employers are insisting that people be able to show what they know and even more importantly, what they can *do*. Are kids developing those durable skills during their high school experience? In too many cases, they are not, which sees them graduating (or dropping out, as is too often the case) into adult life with no real understanding of how the world works. They're leaving school with little awareness of what jobs exist, let alone how they might build the skills needed to launch and sustain a career.

The changes put forth by the authors have been difficult to execute within a system that was designed in and for a different age and a different purpose. Kids are rarely leaving, or being encouraged to look outside of, the confines of the classroom for information about what might come next. In fact, here's the state of work-based learning in our country today. Just 19 states have developed policies or programs above and beyond the minimum federal requirements to ensure access for high-need student groups. Just over half of all states offer financial incentives to offset high school work-based learning costs and encourage businesses to partner with schools to offer work-based learning opportunities[5]. Most states (38) have broad eligibility for student participation in work-based learning. However, eligibility is not the same as a commitment to equitable opportunity. Very few states commit to ensuring that every student can access a variety of work-based-learning experiences. A much broader, systemic commitment to work-based learning, with particular emphasis on real-world learning given what we know about its efficacy, is long overdue.

Simply put, kids in school rarely have the chance to try something new and exciting that might spark the fire of curiosity and motivate them towards a path. In fact, just 2 percent of high school learners we surveyed had completed an internship. And while 79 percent said they were interested in real-world learning experiences, just 34 percent were aware of any such opportunities for students their age.

To reverse this trend, high school students must be given equitable access to robust, high-quality work-based learning programs. Practices that can support successful expansion of work-based learning programs include ensuring equal access for all students, regardless of gender, race, ethnicity, income level, disability status, or academic path, greater awareness among young people, incentives for employer participation, and dedicated funding.

What does this look like in practice? Many states have adopted a "work-based learning coordinator" model and tasked those coordinators with communicating with stakeholders about work-based learning programs and opportunities. Rhode Island's Work-Based Learning Navigator, for example, lets employers post available work-based learning opportunities.

To encourage businesses to participate, some states provide incentives to offset employer costs. New Jersey's Career Accelerator Internship Program provides participating employers with up to 50 percent of wages paid to new interns, amounting to up to $3,000 per student.

In terms of funding, districts and organizations often have difficulty sustaining work-based learning if there isn't a dedicated funding source that makes the program a priority. Massachusetts has a dedicated line-item in the annual state budget to fund high school internships and recently supported the launch of the Work-based Learning Alliance to scale accessibility to virtual work-based learning experiences[6].

With a strong commitment to addressing all challenges, stakeholders can significantly increase the number of available work-based learning opportunities at the high school level. That's why the changes Washor and Boldt put forth in *Learning to Leave* around real-world learning are changes we desperately need to happen now.

Today, perhaps more so than 10 years ago, we don't have the luxury of time to wait around for change to happen in the classroom alone. In fact, I often worry that we are not moving fast enough. It's vital that we embrace "outside" - as the authors assert - as a place where viable and even transformational learning can happen.

It's time to help kids connect school to the outside world, and to start that work much earlier. We must embrace experiential learning that's happening beyond the classroom.

Leaving, in this case, doesn't mean leaving school altogether. It means trying new things and failing safely inside and outside of the classroom; before the stakes become too high and without having to commit to one career path or another before they know themselves. It means the chance to build social capital and a professional network before they make the transition to adulthood. It means connecting students to the real world, so they are more engaged in the work they are doing in school. Yes ... it's okay to leave. And, it's *better* to leave.

Preparing kids to learn and work in this "new normal" economy and workforce - and giving them the skills they'll need to face so many unknowns - must be among the highest national priorities. When schools and communities embrace work-based and experiential real-world learning, as in Big Picture Learning's initiatives, they give local businesses a boost by breathing fresh life into the workforce. They give every parent a ray of hope that, regardless of whether college is part of the plan, their child can create a path to real success finding meaning in work and community. And they give kids the ability to "test and try" before the stakes are too high.

When we commit to looking beyond the classroom and tapping into the vast power of experiential learning, we are making a promise to help every kid, regardless of circumstance, build a path that will afford them hope, purpose, durable skills, and empowerment for the long haul. It's my belief that we're at the beginning of something remarkable.

Ten years from now, I hope readers will revisit this book with a sense of astonishment at how much positive transformation has happened in and around our K-12 schools. Today, I celebrate this book as an optimistic reminder that our vision - a path for every kid - is infinitely achievable when we change the paradigm around what success looks like, and where and how learning can happen. In doing so, we are confident that we can help each young person to navigate the school-to-work journey and bring their future into focus.

__Jean Eddy,__ President and CEO of American Student Assistance® (ASA)

[1]   ECMC Group, Question the Quo. 'Gen Z Teens Want Shorter, More Affordable, Career-Connected Education Pathways.' https://www.questionthequo.org/media/3954/qtq-survey-5-digital-report.pdf

[2]   Consumer News and Business Channel (CNBC). 'Fewer kids are going to college because they say it costs too much.' https://www.cnbc.com/2021/03/14/fewer-kids-going-to-college-because-of-cost.html

[3]   American Student Assistance. 'Best Practices in Youth Work-based Learning: Ensure Broad Eligibility and Widespread Equitable Access'. https://www.asa.org/research/best-practices-in-youth-work-based-learning-ensure-broad-eligibility-and-widespread-equitable-access

[4]   ASA. 'High School Work-based Learning: Best Practices Designed to Improve Career Readiness Outcomes for Today's Youth'. 2022.

[5]   PR Newswire. 'Big Picture Learning and American Student Assistance Partner to Provide Internship Opportunities to Thousands of Students Across the State of California.' https://www.prnewswire.com/news-releases/big-picture-learning-and-american-student-assistance-partner-to-provide-internship-opportunities-to-thousands-of-students-across-the-state-of-california-301364603.html

[6]   ASA. 'High School Work-based Learning: Best Practices Designed to Improve Career Readiness Outcomes for Today's Youth'. 2022.

Every 12 seconds in the U.S., a student drops out of school.

Elliot Washor and **Charles Mojkowski**, both of Big Picture Learning, have a proven solution for stemming the flow: leaving to learn. When students leave the school building to pursue learning opportunities in real world settings, and these experiences are then blended wit[...] learning, the results are life-changing. Motivation, engagem[...] soar. Kids don't ever want to drop out, because suddenly, [...] matters. We can keep kids in school *and* prepare them for [...] tion by delivering authentic learning experiences that mat[...] first step is taking down the barriers between school and t[...] The first step is letting them leave, to learn.

Praise for Leaving to Learn

"Elliot Washor and Charles Mojkowski rightly identify student diseng[...] cause of our nation's dropout crisis. Their solution—'leaving to learn'[...] to the real world of life and work, creating highly engaged learners in[...] strategy—redesigning schools in fundamental ways—is made unders[...] and compelling account."

— LINDA DARLING-HAMMOND, Charles E. D[...]
of Education, Stanford University

"Leaving to Learn puts forth a provocative and powerful argument: [...] of capable young learners are dropping out of high school not becaus[...] schools' expectations, but because schools don't meet theirs. If you're c[...] dropout problem, you owe it to the young people in your life to pick u[...]

— DANIEL H. PINK, author of Drive and A Who[...]

"The authors get inside young people's heads and hearts in order to i[...] how they disengage from learning and often drop out. It's deeper tha[...] authors say, and they are right. Their solution is spot on—start with s[...] to break the cycle of failure. Here's hoping schools will listen."

— PEDRO NOGUERA, Peter L. Agnew Professor[...]
New York University

ELLIOT WASHOR
CHARLES MOJKOWSKI

FOREWORD BY SIR KEN ROBINSON

LEAVING to LEARN

**HOW OUT-OF-SCHOOL LEARNING
INCREASES STUDENT ENGAGEMENT
AND REDUCES DROPOUT RATES**

Preface

In August of 2022, the Co-director of Big Picture Learning Andrew Frishman came to me with an idea. He said, **"El, it's been 10 years since you wrote Leaving to Learn. In that time, we have started many new initiatives that have proven the benefits of leaving to learn and from them have learned a great deal. In the last book you never really had the strong focus on Real-World Learning. I think it is time to go deep as well as broad on what young people are doing out there.**

How about you write a 10-year anniversary book that takes us for a ride in the Wayback Machine and brings us up to the present on what we are doing around the tremendous amount of joyful learning happening outside of school? I know that Jean Eddy, President and CEO of American Student Assistance, is writing a book on Real World Learning that has a focus on policy. Could this book be the practical accompaniment to hers that takes what we've done in practice and connects it to policy?"

Given all we and others have done up to and through COVID and now dealing with the possibilities of "new normals", it didn't take much time for me to realize that combining this book on principles and practice with Jean Eddy's on policy was a great idea so, I said to Andrew, "Yes, let's do it." Two days later, we were on a Zoom with American Student Assistance (ASA), with Andrew pitching the idea of a 10-year update on *Leaving to Learn.* The folks at ASA loved it. That's how this book got its start. I am very grateful to Andrew and ASA for this opportunity to share how we are *Learning to Leave* by getting "inside the outside" with insights into New Ways, New Forms and New Measures that together transform learning and learners as well as schools, youth development organizations and industry.

Albert Einstein escaped Germany in 1933 to pursue his research at Princeton, where he taught a course. There is a story, perhaps apocryphal, but nonetheless illuminating, that when he distributed the questions for the final exam, one student observed:

Professor Einstein, these are the same questions you gave out last semester." "Yes," Einstein replied, "the same questions. But the answers are different this year."

Einstein's response said much about the state of theoretical physics in the anxious decade before WWII, and about our present situation coming out of COVID. His response is also a strong encouragement to look back at the "answers" we gave in *Leaving to Learn* (LTL) and to present this year's "answers" in *Learning to Leave* (L2L) about what we have learned over the ten years since Charlie and I wrote LTL.

I need to mention and to thank Charlie Mojkowski (Mojo) who has been on the Big Picture Learning journey since Dennis and I started it back in Providence in 1995. Unfortunately, Charlie was not available to work with me on this new book, but I have been able to team up with Professor Scott Boldt who has known and been writing about our work since the late 90s. Over the past five years, Scott and a team of researchers have evaluated our initiatives and programs that are our New Ways, New Forms and New Measures for learning. I must also give a shout out to Kapua Chandler, Danique Dolly, Carrie Ferguson, Anthonette Peña, Charlie Plant, Andrea Purcell and Beth White who all contributed to this book.

Finally, I have to acknowledge the sudden passing of Sir Ken Robinson which hit many of us very hard. His voice was so important to our work and he graciously added it to the Foreword in LTL. If he were with us now, I'm sure his friendship, love and voice would have made our work even more meaningful. This is our attempt to keep the movement alive and thriving for all of our youth especially, for those who have the hardest obstacles to overcome as they become. As Duke Ellington always said, "Love you madly!".

Elliot Washor

Acknowledgements

Big Picture Learniing's Co-directors, Carlos Moreno and Andrew Frishman, continue to amaze all of us through their dedication, hard work and leadership of the new initiatives described in this book and so much more, in turning practice into policy for all youth regardless of demographics. Un millón de gracias.

Dennis Littky and Elliot have been working together for 52 years - what more can be said? M.R. Brezler, as per usual, has contributed a tremendous amount in helping us get this book over the finish line - many thanks.

All of the BPL staff, we thank you for making sure the work continues and develops as New Ways, New Forms and New Measures emerge.

We are grateful to ASA for all of their support and encouragement. We also want to acknowledge our gratitude to Harbor Freight Tools for Schools, to Bo Stjerne Thomsen of the LEGO Foundation, and to Pam Roy, friend and co-founder of B-Unbound.

Viv White is the dynamic leader of Big Picture in Australia, and it has been through her efforts and that of her team that we have the amazing New Measure of the International Big Picture Learning Credential (IBPLC).

We hope we don't leave anyone out as we thank the following people for helping us in various and important ways in the preparation of this manuscript: Sophie Boldt, Peter Hall Jones, Andrea Purcell, Ian Robinson and Emma Soye.

As it turns out, both of our wives are Irish. Since we first met them, Darlene and Hilary have been showing us new ways and new forms of how to be, and they continue to develop new measures to keep our feet planted firmly on the ground and in love.

Introduction

Over the past 10 years, our world has gone through major tectonic shifts, from the arts to the sciences, and from climate change and race relations, to disease and technology. All of these shifts are interconnected. You can start anywhere, but in a brief moment all these issues start coming into view.

All of these impact our world, nation, communities and youth. Yet, much of the world for young people, when they are with adults, remains confined within the four walls of the school, community center, home or within the four sides of a screen. In school, youth experience is marked not by engaging in the challenges facing our world but by the same narrow band of standards espousing "what is smart" (based on graduation requirements, the common core or the canon you need to know) with little emphasis on "how you are smart", how you are engaging with the world and on how you can contribute to addressing the needs of your community, country and our planet.

The focus on standardization and school-based standards inevitably leads to, in fact it demands, regulation (of time, relationships, place and experience), conformity to what is prescribed by the curriculum, and compliance with the expectations and activities deemed necessary to obtain the information needed to perform well on tests. Now more than ever our children's world keeps shrinking to ongoing and often trivial text and images on a screen. Often the sole purpose of the tools, regulations and technologies in school is to keep students locked in and (effectively) locked up. They are in a world of over-regulation that narrows the places and spaces of where and how learning is allowed to happen, and sets standards that are primarily (and often only) relevant for school and advancing to another level of schooling.

Big Picture Learning (BPL), American Student Assistance (ASA) and others have worked against these policies and practices of regulation, not because we are mavericks who like rebelling against authority, but because the culture and patterns of schooling are undermining learning, and maintaining and even increasing inequities. This does not serve most of our children well and even harms many children who leave school without confidence, certification, useful skills and meaningful prospects.

Over the past 30 years, I have done a weekly newsletter called TGIF that addresses these issues through the practices in our schools and communities.

I guess I was a blogger before blogging. Also, in the past ten years I've written a series of articles in homage to one of my mentors, Seymour Sarason, who always asked the question: What do you mean by learning? Excerpts from the TGIFs and articles will be scattered throughout this book to show how, over the ten years since LTL was written, our work on **how** to learn to leave has progressed. Here's the first example that deals with where we are at present.

TGIF

*A very few calls on Memorial Day Monday gave me the time to read a book Viv White, the Executive Director of Big Picture Australia, recently sent me. **Sand Talk: How Indigenous Thinking Can Save the World** (2019), by Tyson Yunkaporta, is a gem. Tyson's explanation of the history of public schooling takes us through how imperialism (the Prussian System) and modern globalization used techniques similar to how animals were domesticated. It is just one quick example I'll share here.*

1 *Separate the young from their parents in the daylight hours*

2 *Confine them in an enclosed space with limited stimulation or access to natural habitat*

3 *Use rewards and punishments to force them to comply with purposeless tasks.*

*There's lots of new language in **Sand Talk**, or rather, language translated from indigenous to modern. Tyson creates words like 'extra-cognitive' instead of non-cognitive. Through his yarnings, Tyson delves into different ways of knowing that are sentient, tacit and part of cultural capital. Tyson wrote a book that is fun, dynamic and shows ways to get to a sustainable future. Definitely worth seeing how our actions fit and play out in what Tyson is doing and how we can change.*

***Note:** Real-World Learning (RWL) is the antidote to the system Tyson describes. In RWL the entire community is the school.*

Inside the Outside

This book is all about real-world learning (RWL) and about getting deeply inside the outside where young people are engaged with adults around their interests in search of doing things that matter to them that give their life meaning. The *Learning to Leave* (L2L) sequel builds on the foundation we provided in LTL and presents the New Ways, New Forms and New Measures that have emerged from our practices of RWL in the workplace and community.

In LTL we discussed why The Deeper Four are reasons students are not engaging in school which show that we have met the enemy and he is us (i.e., the adults in the system and our system that prevents or inhibits student engagement and leads youth to dropout). We also spent a great deal of time on the **10 Expectations** which, our experience suggested, students have of schools, but those expectations are not present in the same way in RWL. The 10 Expectations only present themselves when a school gets involved in RWL otherwise they are self-assessments. In L2L we will address how schools can get involved in RWL, and, just as important, how they should not. We do this in the hopes that schools pay attention to the potential of getting students out and crediting the incredible things youth are doing in the real world. We call this Bringing the Outside Inside and Getting the Inside Outside.

We hope that schools take RWL very seriously, but up to now they have not, and our children and system are the worse for this. It is our contention that schools make it more difficult to take advantage of RWL because of the ways, forms and measures of the education system that dictate what is smart and who is smart. This manifests itself in, but is not limited to, race, class and gender.

RWL has tremendous untapped potential for what schools and community centers must become in order to do what they say they do in their mission and vision statements. And, far more than words, we have put into action New Ways, New Forms and New Measures that will educe and spark young people to search and work on who they are and who they want to become.

Big Picture Learning (BPL)

Before we move on, there is a need to set out the background and the context of Big Picture Learning which informs, guides, and provides the organization and infrastructure for all the work we have been doing on leaving to learn. Although Dennis Littky and I are the co-founders of BPL, it really was a community of contributors that set up Big Picture Company, including Keith Olivera, Zeylane Walker-Cabral, Julie Gainsburg, Sanna Randolph, Danique Dolly, Elaine Hackney, Brian Mills, Rhode Island Commissioner Peter

McWalter, families and our advisors and dramateurs Deborah Meier, Ted Sizer, Howard Fuller, Seymour Sarason and Herb Kohl.

In fact, we called it Big Picture Company in the beginning not because we were a business but because we wanted to emphasize that education and learning is about being in company with others in the school and in the community - wherever your interests take you. One of our early slogans was "Education is everyone's business". We felt that many people

The **BIG** Four

Academic Failure

—

Behavior

—

Life Events

—

Disinterest

Not Mattering

—

Not Fitting In

—

Unrecognized Talents & Interests

—

Restrictions

The **DEEPER** Four

wrongly associated learning with something that happens only in school and college when you have a teacher. Instead, we always saw that learning is happening everywhere, formally and informally, in the home, school, streets, communities and in third spaces where we gather. Larry Cremin eloquently wrote about this in his book *Public Education* (1976), strongly suggesting that schools take advantage of all these places where learning is happening.

BPL started in Providence, Rhode Island in 1995, and from the beginning we saw it as part of a movement for change, a way to transform schools that brought together all our ideas about education and learning. You could say that we built it on innovative educational principles with a primary focus on learning - in and out of school. Some of where it came from was us playing out, "What if we didn't know what a school was - how would we design one?"

And how can we keep the design flexible so that when we learn how to do things better, the school can change? This led us to designing the schools around what is known now as the **10 Distinguishers.**

Our basic practice and philosophy of learning centers around Interests, Relationships and Practice in real life situations, because we know that learning happens best when interests, relationships, and practice are woven together. People learn more quickly, more deeply, more comprehensively, and more meaningfully when they are pursuing their interests with skilled people who know them and let them practice, play, make mistakes, start over again, ask more questions, test things out and then show what they can do - not tested on how smart they are in a lab-like setting. I like the phrase "muddling through, mingling with, mattering to" to capture how most of us learn most of the time.

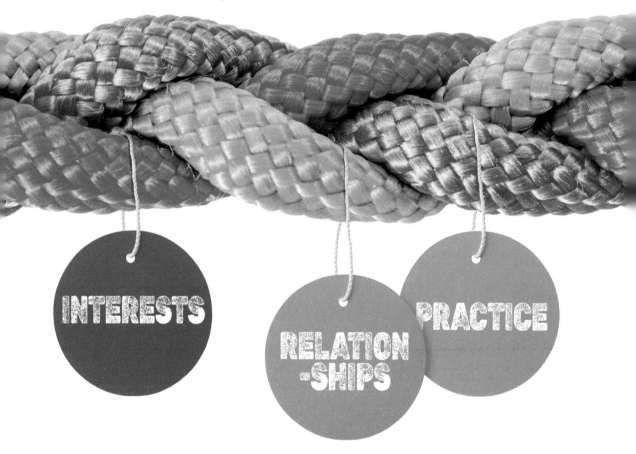

The **10** Distinguishers

PARENT AND FAMILY ENGAGEMENT

Parents are welcome and valued members of the school community and play a proactive role in their children's learning, collaborating in the planning and assessment of student work. They use their assets to support the work of the school, and often play an integral role in building relationships with potential LTI mentors.

LEADERSHIP

Leadership is shared and spread between a strong, visionary principal; a dedicated, responsible team of advisors and other staff; and students. The community functions as a democracy. A pervasive sense of shared ownership drives a positive culture dedicated to ongoing improvement.

ONE STUDENT AT A TIME

The entire learning experience is personal to each student. Personal learning plans expand beyond mere academic work and involve looking at each student holistically.

SCHOOL CULTURE

In Big Picture schools, there is palpable trust, respect and equality between and among students and adults. Students take leadership roles in the school, and teamwork defines the adult culture. Student voice is valued in the school decision making process and visitors are struck by the ease with which students interact with adults.

ADVISORY STRUCTURE

Advisory is the core organizational and relational structure of a Big Picture Learning school, its heart and soul, often described as a 'second family' by students. Students stay with an advisor and a group of fellow classmates for years, building close personal relationships that last a lifetime.

POSTSECONDARY PLANNING

Students develop plans that contribute to their future success - be it through college, trades, schools, travel, the military, or the workforce.

AUTHENTIC ASSESSMENT

Students are assessed not by tests, but by public displays of learning that track growth and progress in the student's area of interest. Assessment criteria are based on each student and the real world standards of a project. Students present multiple exhibitions each year and discuss their learning growth with staff, parents, peers, and mentors.

PROFESSIONAL DEVELOPMENT

Regular advisor PD is conducted at each school by principals, other school staff, and BPL staff and coaches. A Big Picture School is a community of lifelong learners who embrace continuous improvement.

LEARNING THROUGH INTERESTS AND INTERNSHIPS (LTIs)

Real world learning is best accomplished in the real world. Big Picture students intern - often twice a week for an entire school day - with experts in their field of interest, completing authentic projects and gaining experience and exposure to how their interests intersect with the real world.

SCHOOL ORGANIZATION

Schools are organized around a culture of collaboration and communication. They are not bound by the structures of buildings, schedules, bells, or calendars. There is an interdependence between school and community.

The learning we gained from our practice is why BPL has a personal curriculum for each student built on and around their needs and wants, interests and passions, and the things they find out that give their life meaning. It is also why we have an advisory structure where the advisor (teacher) really knows the learners and they know each other. Our schools are not huge because you are not known, and you don't know everybody, where there are 1,500 or 5,000 people. That said, The Met in Providence is 900 students BUT we broke the entire school into six small schools. Four of them on one campus (www.themethighschool.org). Form follows function.

One of the main principles or rather, our motto, is "One-Student-at-a-Time-in-a-Community" which recognizes that every student brings her/his unique abilities, interests, needs, circumstances, and context into school and into their learning. Each student is part of an advisory, a learning community, with an advisor guiding them and, navigating with them, to identify their needs and explore their interests. Learning plans and goals for each student make learning personal, engaging, and relevant along with the participation of families and mentors. Positive student interests, whatever they may be, are the context for their learning. The student is the curriculum and the entire community (their town, their city) is the school - education is everyone's business. Form follows function.

A student-driven curriculum is developed around real-world experiences and standards. As distinct from conventional schooling with the focus on a prescribed curriculum and academic testing in the school, BPL is unconventional and outward looking. Interest-driven explorations and internships are key to the BPL approach and establish the context for learning where the disciplines are integrated with their interests. Mentorship in a real-world setting offers students access to skilled adults and therefore to deep and sustained learning and skill development in fields in which they are committed and passionate. All students are challenged to pursue their interests and are supported by a community of educators, professionals, peers, and family members. Form follows function.

BPL schools support the concept of leaving to learn because it enables the powerful learning that occurs when students leave their school as part of the school program to expand and deepen their learning, to get exposure to new practices, ideas, people and opportunities, and to learn through their interests in the best places where those interests are happening - in real-world settings and workplaces in relationship with adults. Typically, BPL high school students are out of school two days a week; they might be doing informational interviews, a shadow day with somebody doing a job that they are curious about, attending a course at a community college, organizing a community service project, spending time with their mentor at their internship or travelling near and far - it all depends on their interests and where they can explore and pursue them. Form follows ... that's getting a bit repetitive, but it's true. Our New Ways of applying learning theory demanded and led to New Forms and to New Measures. The Forms and Measures followed the Ways which are the functions. And in the way infants learn, we first grasped the world then figured out the language and with Hand, Heart, Head and Health interplaying and meshing together we moved forward.

Discontent with Content

From the work we have done over decades, it is obvious that content and instruction are not the issues we want to focus on. They both happen in the context of what the learner wants to learn and what the adults who know them well advise them as their next steps in instruction of skills and content. The issue in learning anything is how to approach the content, whatever it is, through three things - a student's interests, the relationship between the adult and student, and the place where the relationship or where the learning takes place.

If a child is to keep alive his [or her] inborn sense of wonder, he [or she] needs the companionship of at least one adult who can share it, rediscovering with him the joy, excitement and mystery of the world we live in."

Rachel Carson 1956, 27

Underlying these essential BPL elements is attention to personal relationships when people know each other closely and harness that relationship to advance learning and growth. It is these sustained, meaningful relationships that create the context for high expectations and appropriate support; individual experience allows room for autonomy and choices. The school's success depends on knowing how to deepen personal relationships while simultaneously diversifying each student's learning experiences both in and outside of school.

We're not sure of why so many schools and programs miss the connections of learning through student interests, learning through relationships, and learning through place, but they are everywhere in biography and in research. Researcher Benjamin Bloom, in *Developing Talent in Young People* (1985), found that schools are not very good at spotting or developing talent. Bloom studied young people who excelled in the arts, sciences, sports, and games and found a typical pattern.

1   **These young people had an interest and some talent they wanted to pursue;**

2   **a mentor of some sort told them and their parents early on they had some talent;**

3   **the young people made the decision to pursue their talents and, as they improved, they attracted better mentors and coaches.**

Lauren Sosniak, Bloom's researcher-colleague, sadly concluded, "Our current methods of instruction may be quite inappropriate for the long-term development of talent. We have a tendency, it seems, to emphasize momentary attentiveness, the acquisition of quickly acquired and simplistic skills, and immediate success" (Sosniak 1989, 288). We agree and think it's because we are hyper-focused on the content and not the process, thinking anyone and everyone can learn if we have the right materials, as the way to equity. Are we too focused on the score and not the game?

Learning from Practice

Too many young people are not thriving in school and in their communities, or they are barely surviving, or they have decided to disengage. BPL has been learning with learners of all ages, all across the country and the world for coming up to 30 years. You can find BPL in kindergartens, elementary schools, middle schools, but predominantly in high schools. We are in the community where young people are at (b-unbound.org), and we are even in college with College Unbound (collegeunbound.edu).

From India to Italy and Israel, Barbados to Belize, Kenya to Canada and Kazakhstan, the Netherlands to New Zealand, Australia to the UK, BPL has grown into an international network of schools and learning environments serving approximately 12,000 students and youth in nearly 30 states and an additional 75+ schools and learning centers in 13 countries with upwards of 35,000 young people. The approach of BPL from K-College and beyond is to operate flexibly and in response to the needs of each learner and the community in which she or he is situated.

In these last 10 years, not only have we grown in size but we have also organically grown to what anthropologist Tim Ingold calls a "meshwork" where our work with one another has twists and turns. As Gaudi said, "there are no straight lines in nature". BPL has schools where together we learn from our experiences by muddling through to New Ways, New Forms and New Measures that emerge to then influence our practice and change policy. We have continued to be practitioners that change policy through our practices. Like Buckminster Fuller, we are not about reforming a system because the framework to be reformed relies on much that does not work. Rather we forge and muddle through to New Ways and New Forms leading to New Measures around what matters and has meaning to students, parents, schools. communities, colleges, and employers.

Avanti

The format of this book opens with where we've been over the past decade in the context of real-world learning, how we have been learning to leave better, and indicating where we are going to have RWL transform education. Chapter One is called **Looking Back** and we present our learning from our practices in the 10 years since LTL was written since, so much has evolved. We have developed New Ways, New Forms and New Measures in our work and these are critical for RWL to transform education. In Chapter One, we set out our rationale for making real-world leaving to learn opportunities available to every student and young person in school or in the community. We will talk about the spread of leaving to learn and how work on the edge can move to the center of the education system and transform it.

New Ways is the title of Chapter Two because in this chapter we outline the key elements of working on our emerging New Ways, or muddling through towards them, that lead to New Forms, including our practices of New Measures of assessment that vet and validate the rightness of those ways and forms. We believe that these New Ways will help educators provide for equity in their learning opportunities and the learning environments they create for all students. These New Ways are the function that the form follows.

In Chapter Three we present the **New Forms** of BPL; the programs and practices that demonstrate the power of leaving to learn and show how we have been learning to leave. The initiatives are developed around New Ways of facilitating RWL (interests-relationships-practice). The New Forms include B-Unbound, the Harbor Freight Fellows Initiative, Project InSight and Los Angeles Leaves to Learn which are all facilitated by the digital platform ImBlaze.

Chapter Four, **New Measures,** presents the International Big Picture Learning Credential (IBPLC), the new skilled trades 311 Credential, and BPLiving, New Measures on health and well-being that are preventative and prerequisites for sustained and meaningful learning for both physical and mental health together - not separate. We will describe how these Measures were developed during and through COVID and highlight their growth. We will advocate against traditional, standardized testing as the only way in which a person's smartness can be assessed and as the main route for accessing postsecondary education, apprenticeships and more meaningful employment. The New Measures are breakthrough ways of assessing student learning and crediting and recognizing competencies and learning that are relevant for college, employment and having a good life.

Chapter Five is **Looking Ahead** and our emphasis here is on policy and community, and how to scale and sustain the New Ways, Forms and Measures. Julie Lammers of ASA shares their policy pieces in this chapter which helps us understand how more and more learners are able to engage in RWL connected to their interests with supportive adults and then be credited for it. We believe that policy has to follow practice rather than policy dictating or limiting practice.

 TGIF

*Here's another way of looking at the problem of standards. Are we All for One or One for All or are we All for each and everyone of us? Or are we All for only one way? Coincidently, the book I read this week was **What Can a Body Do? How We Meet the Built World (2020)** by Sarah Hendren. What emerges in the book are the hidden assumptions on which the everyday environment is built when a body doesn't fit the built world, hence, the use of the word 'misfit' in this book. Sarah Hendren's history of everyday objects and the abstract concepts of time and navigation/proprioception lead us into how the world was and is shaped around what is deemed normal. There are some frightening histories exposed here around the role of eugenics in our measurement system and where our systems are today with regards to race, gender and class.*

With all of this in mind and given that so many of us will develop a disability over our lifetime, a question becomes: Are we about All for One measures, acknowledging that we are all different or are we only developing One for All measures of quality and purpose? Our education system and all of our other systems are built on efficiency, acceleration and being less costly. But acceleration is a trend and not a law, and slowness, not speed, is fundamental to quality. Anytime

you can't do something fast enough, you are deemed not able and labeled disabled or a misfit. Whether it is crossing a street in a certain amount of time or keeping up with the group while reading a book or doing math problems, the industrial age brought measures of success in doing everything by the clock. In this way, Sarah Hendren discusses the rise of normalcy as a modern standard of measure and "the clock as the highest judge of our moral and economic value."

The photo above was taken during World War II at 10 East 40th Street in Manhattan. It is my Uncle Gabe and his brother Harold behind the counter. I don't know the other people at their cigar/news stand. When I was a kid, I would take the train to visit my uncles in this building which at one time was the tallest building in the world, and the elevator operator would let me shut the expandable elevator gates and then, slide the elevator control handle to the left and off we went to the top floor. My friends and I would go up on the roof, look out on the city, and eat Mary Janes and Bit-O-Honeys that my uncles gave us.

Every time I'm in NYC, I go into this building. The cigar stand is no longer there but the space still delineates where it was. I'm telling this story because Harold had tuberculosis as an infant and the doctors performed some type of surgery on him that made him small, walk with a limp and hunch his back. My Uncle Gabe never finished the third grade. Both of these men were highly literate. Gabe read at least a book a week, taking books out from the New York City Public Library which was right across 5th Ave on 40th Street. As a child, Harold was put into schools where they didn't want to look at kids who looked different. This was the vocational schools in NYC.

Uncle Harold went to Westinghouse High School. It was the same school that Busta Rhymes, Lil' Kim, Biggie Smalls and Jay-Z went and were put there albeit for different but similar reasons (i.e., sorted out of the mainstream - misfits). Despite the odds, Harold figured out how to graduate high school and college. Harold lived above Gabe and collected paperback books. The books were stacked in every room, floor to ceiling and three rows thick. He had thousands of books and read every one of them. Once in a while you could hear some rows of books topple down from Gabe's apartment below.

As a kid, I was a reluctant reader. I actually couldn't read a book until 7th grade. What I did read even with great difficulty were comics, but in college whenever I needed a book for research, my go-to place was Harold's apartment. He always had something.

The other part of this story is that every Saturday, I would go somewhere in NYC with my Uncle Gabe. When the weather was not so good, we would go to a museum. When it was good, we were off to Coney Island and at

some point, in the day, we would find Harold. Harold did two things at Coney Island - walk the boardwalk and hangout with his crew who, like Harold, looked different. They were missing arms, legs, ears, noses and had other disfigurements. I was this little kid with my uncles and was just there. I remember everyone was nice but this group was not about a little kid. These folks were part of a community, some of whom worked in the Side Shows and were just hanging out off-hours.

I was reminded about all of this because of an interview question asked of me about how I came to make a school like The Met in Providence. I said I give a different set of responses almost every time and that it is really a difficult question but this time because of Sarah Hendren's book, Uncle Gabe and Uncle Harold became part of the response. I did so much of my learning outside of school and when inside, I challenged almost everything being taught to me because I had different norms and different answers that I knew were more accurate than what I was being taught in school. This is real-world learning.

We want this book to be a place that you visit, a space where you can be inspired and a base where you return to consider and reconsider your practice, your policies - your ways, forms and measures. Here you will meet students, youth, parents, mentors and educators who do this work and exemplify the New Ways, New Forms and New Measures in their own words. We hope you enjoy the journey and that it leads you to engage in the RWL that is needed to transform education.

Chapter One

Looking Back

When I go into any school, when I get a chance to talk to a student, I always try to ask some questions that tell me if what they are doing is real or fake; sometimes I just ask them that - ***"Is what you're doing here real or fake?"***, and they tell you without hesitation and they tell you why it is one way or the other.

Another good question - ***"Is this your work or school work?"***, and that matters because when you are doing "your work", you are engaged, interested and learning; when you're doing somebody else's work, you are usually less engaged, you may not be interested at all and there's a good chance there's not much valuable learning going on.

I ask another question of students when they've been doing something or if they are showing me some of their work: ***"How do you think you did?"***. Most of the time in schools nobody asks students how they did. They tell them how they did. We have to remind ourselves that self-assessment is one of the most powerful forms of assessment (and it gives a great insight into learning) and is not used nearly enough in schools. If it matters they will tell you - "I have to read these 5 books, meet these people, travel to these places, take these three courses, find a mentor" - the list will go on and on.

Another question for students is, ***"What do you want to get better at?"***, because it uncovers a bit of self-assessment, it can indicate how interested they are in something, and it may reveal a different and deeper interest. It's not necessarily that the student is pursuing an interest that leads to a career or deep passion, but because they're interested in something, what they want to get better at might be digressions around those bigger interests, where they can also pick up a particular skill set.

If answers to my questions show that what students are doing is real for them, their assessments are honest, and they want to get better by taking next steps, I'm confident that they are learning and developing because when something is real to you, it matters. RWL engages students, and it is highly likely that you

are going to stay in a place and be all-in if you're engaged in something you care about, if you have a good relationship with the people you are learning from and working with, and if you're learning more about it and able to put that learning into practice in authentic ways. These truths are evident in Director of Harbor Freight Fellows Charlie Plant's story of Harbor Freight Fellow, Esteban Gonzalez.

 Esteban

Esteban Gonzalez was a student of Career and Technical Eduction (CTE) Power Mechanics teacher Eric Dyer, in Woodland California. Woodland's an agricultural town - the tomato capitol of America, miles and miles of almond groves and rice fields. It's a salt of the earth, working town. Eric Dyer had been the bedrock of Woodland High School's CTE and Future Farmers of America (FFA) programs for over 30 years when he nominated Esteban to be a Harbor Freight Fellow. Eric knew Esteban to be a talented, conscientious student when working with his hands in his classes. He also knew that Esteban struggled with school and was very close to leaving school to go to work, and that Esteban was struggling with who he was, what was his path in life. Esteban just knew he loved working with his hands and didn't love school. He was lost.

Even in Woodland, kids not aspiring to college were tacitly relegated to second class status. In his gut, Esteban knew college was not for him, at least not at that point in his life. Eric connected him with Jim Bannister as a mentor for his Fellowship. Jim owns Truck Mixer Supply in Woodland, repairing and doing routine maintenance on those huge cement mixer trucks you see rolling down the road. His is the only such facility from the central valley up to the Pacific Northwest - a big deal in the cement mixer world. Esteban took to the work like a duck to water. Within a very short time he was working on the critical systems on those heavy equipment monsters, in particular the hydraulic systems.

Jim couldn't have been more impressed and happier with Esteban. He hired him and Esteban worked with Jim for several years. It's a small community and word of Esteban's skill got around. A national heavy agricultural equipment company, Holt Agricultural Solutions, made an offer to Esteban that he couldn't refuse. Esteban went on to become a certified, top level heavy equipment mechanic for all aspects of the agricultural equipment industry, something Jim couldn't offer Esteban in his business. Esteban has been sent all around the country for Holt - both working at different dealerships, and gaining specialized training. Jim continues to be a supportive mentor to Esteban, as does his CTE teacher, Eric Dyer.

The result of their support, and of Esteban's Harbor Freight Fellowship, is that Esteban has a secure place in the professional world, self-respect and financial security and a bright future. He is poised to be able to start a family, own his own home, and has already mentored other Harbor Freight Fellows. And it all started with Eric Dyer placing him in a Harbor Freight Fellowship, with a mentor, around work that he loved to do, in the real world, doing real work. It can't be that simple ... but it is.

Expectations

When *Leaving to Learn* was written 10 years ago, our focus was on demonstrating how out-of-school learning increases student engagement and reduces dropout rates. In the book, the case was made for the importance of leaving (school) to learn in view of the Big Four predictors of school dropout cited in the literature (academic failure, student behavior, life events and disinterest) as well as the Deeper Four reasons highlighted by young people (not mattering, not fitting in, not having talents and interests recognized, and not being able to do things because of school restrictions). We put forward 10 student expectations that we believed were indispensable conditions that schools must provide if they are to engage students. What we have learned over these past 10 years is that while our views hold up in practice, it is even simpler than the way we stated it when it comes to initiatives in and outside of school. To use Buckminster Fuller's language we are 'doing more with less' - a sure sign of moving toward a healthier more robust learning environment.

Ten years ago, **setting high expectations for students** from the adult perspective was all the buzz. There was that belief (partly true) that if I have high expectations of you, then you will learn more and do better, but if I expect little of you or that you will fail, it is like a self-fulfilling prophecy. LTL had a very different take on "expectations" and made the case for leaving to learn as a means of addressing students' expectations rather than adult expectations of them. The 10 Expectations still hold, especially in developing a whole school culture, but through our practice and doing an expansive review of the research we started to focus on Interests-Relationships-Practice. The intertwining of these three principles for learning, which correspond to the 10 Expectations, are the ways our initiatives provide RWL for both schools and youth development organizations.

10 Student Expectations

Interests

- **Relevance:** do I find what the school is teaching to be relevant to my interests?
- **Choice:** do I have real choices about what, when, and how I will learn and demonstrate my competence?
- **Time:** do I have sufficient time to learn at my own pace?
- **Timing:** can I pursue my learning out of the standard sequence?

Relationships

- **Relationships:** do my teachers and others who might serve as my teachers know about me (my culture, my identity) and my interests and talents?
- **Authenticity:** is the learning and work I do regarded as significant outside school by experts, family, community, and employers?

Practice

- **Application:** do I have opportunities to apply what I am learning in real-world settings and contexts?
- **Play:** do I have opportunities to explore - and to make mistakes and learn from them - without being branded a failure?
- **Practice:** do I have opportunities to engage in deep and sustained practice of those skills I want to learn?
- **Challenge:** do I feel appropriately challenged in my learning and work?

WITH and WANT

To this point, in LTL we spent time on explaining a Seymour Sarason concept called **productive learning,** starting where students are at and what they **want** to learn. Over these years we have moved from "productive learning" to **WITH and WANT.** Productive learning, as Seymour says, is that learning that you want to do. Now, we are combining it with WITH; who you are learning with. We have learned that this combination of with and want is very important. WITH and WANT together in a real-world setting is the intertwining of Interests-Relationships-Practice which has been shown to be extraordinarily powerful both in the research and in practice for engaging learners and making learning stick. Excerpts from an article written by Elliot portray these ideas well.

In 1936 Bud Abbott and Lou Costello introduced to a national audience one of the greatest comedy routines in vaudeville history - "Who's on first?". The routine is beloved by many for its well-orchestrated series of hilarious misunderstandings resulting from both men talking right by one another. Applying this bewildering baseball skit from the world of entertainment to the realities of education, we are reminded that schools and the workplace are also talking by one another, failing to exploit the power of who you know in concert with what you know to achieve success.

*What can be gleaned from the message that Bud and Lou were sending out? In Julia Freeland Fisher's book, **Who You Know: Unlocking Innovations that Expand Students' Networks (2018)** she points out how much who you know matters in the*

world. Taking things a step further, could it be that What and Who are the dynamic player combo that is missing in education? In the world of education, "What" has been on first for a very long time. Isn't it time we come to some reconciliation around connecting who and what and measure them together as part of school and how we learn? We need to stop pretending that who you know doesn't count. Certainly, everyone in the world at-large thinks "who you know" or, more significantly, "who knows you know what you know" is important. Examples abound. Now take this a step further, where the what is "what you want to learn" and - watch out!

*The business literature is replete with articles on the power of deep and broad connections and relationships. Organizations invest millions in building learning networks. In academia, who you know and who knows you know often lead to pathways to publishing and admissions to graduate schools. Anthropologist Étienne Wenger, in his classic, **Communities of Practice: Learning, Meaning, and Identity (1998),** designated social behavior in networks and communities as a major source of learning, not just knowing what but also knowing who.*

*Parents play key roles in supporting their children's interests by getting them coaching, internships and work. Parents connect their children through their interests to people who can help them get better and whom they want to be around. Just take a look at the legacies in sports, medicine, business, the arts, the trades and sciences that was highlighted in the research of Benjamin Bloom and Lauren Sosniak on **Developing Talent in Young People (1985).***

In a world where we are educating all children across race, class, gender, and children with different abilities, isn't access to "who knows you know what you know" an equity issue?

We can easily see that gaining access to who, combined with what you are interested in, should not be left only to certain families, groups, schools and colleges with powerful access to alums and the job market. What can be done? Educators continue to focus exclusively on all manner of whats - grades, standardized test scores, diplomas, and certifications - as determining access to learning and work opportunities with little attention to the potential melding of what and who.

The data on creating more equitable schools have plateaued. An article by Lauren Camera in US NEWS and World Report (2016) showed that "using current data it is estimated that if the achievement gaps continue to close at its current incremental rate, it will take about two and a half centuries before the black-white math gap closes and over one and a half centuries until the reading gap closes." Sadly, Julia Freeland Fisher (2018) writes: "Traditional schools' batch-processing models of instruction, by their very design, tend to reward centralized, standardized approaches to the detriment of student-centered and community-based approaches. Big Picture Learning's approach simply does not square with the traditional system's value proposition and the architecture that supports it" (98).

In BPL schools, through our practice and research, we have learned that what a student is interested in and who must be connected and measured. Most recently, our New Forms provide additional evidence of the what-who (want and with) connections that reach beyond our schools and into the workplace. Bud and Lou's skit continues to resonate, reminding us how important it is for educators, in their teaching and assessments, to employ the dynamic combination of what and who to provide

for all our students the opportunities they need to thrive in their lifelong learning and careers. Who-with-what provides the currency to get to where they want to go. Without this reckoning only the few will continue to benefit from either what or who.

In his book in 2009 and in his keynote address at our BPL conference in 2016, the late Sir Ken Robinson reminded us how discovering talents and passions transforms people's lives. He encouraged us to continue enabling youth to pursue their interests. In our BPL schools, prominence is placed on "Learning Through Interest" where all students have a personal learning plan and are supported to access and connect to adults with similar interests to learn, practice, and develop relevant competencies in a RWL environment.

New Ways, New Forms, New Measures

RWL opportunities can be incorporated into all schools and they can also be offered to young people who are not in schools. Done in a way we are describing, RWL has the potential to shift the locus of control and agency to young people. We don't need schools to do this work, but it will help. Furthermore, in LTL we looked past the identified systemic reasons why students are disengaged and dropping out from school and focused on how to increase motivation and engagement in learning by starting with what students want to learn and who they want to learn with. We are continuing to make the case, but here in L2L, we are addressing what we have been doing in the realm of New Ways, New Forms and New Measures.

Since LTL was written in 2013, a lot has happened with respect to RWL with growing recognition of its importance for all young people as part of their total learning experience. We have learned a lot that can contribute to understanding RWL practice and policy. We have found New Ways to do the work that have led to New Forms and New Measures. Our practice has changed and out of that enlightenment our language to describe the practice has changed.

We believe that "form follows function", so in our case, "function" is the New Ways we will present in Chapter Three. The 10 Expectations in LTL were our New Ways for our schools and they produced New Forms for schooling such as Person Learning Plans, Real-World Learning, Learning Through Interests, Student Exhibitions and Portfolios - all part of the 10 Distinguishers of BPL, the New Forms.

Following LTL, we continued to research the best programs in Career and Technical Education (CTE) and in schools, and we found that the new (and best) ways were focused on Interests-Relationships-Practice which provide the best educational context for learning to take place and for youth to discover meaningful pursuits and meaning for their lives. Interests-Relationships-Practice have become the bedrock of the New Forms (Chapter Four) which are our programs and initiatives that are not schools but can be part of school or lived and used outside of school.

What we have also learned is that we have to spend time on other new ways outside of our work that have developed in the last 10 years. One of these is within the DIY movement. Over time, DIY learning resources have changed from where before they were text, diagrams and images (or audio) to now where they are videos both from experts and people en masse who know how to do a simple task or procedure. This is a new way but buyer beware! DIYs can fall short and fool people into thinking they really are plumbers, electricians, doctors, pilots, etc.

What is missing in the new DIY is the practice and the mentorship - the commitment over time to a craft, trade or skill that highly skilled crafts and tradespeople and professionals have acquired and mastered over a lifetime. It is that quality that they bring to their work that gives their lives meaning and plays a large role in how they mentor novices prepared to make a similar commitment. This matters a great deal and highlights the need for the New Measures (Chapter Five) that we have introduced, because we are talking about getting young people to find meaning in their lives through their interests where they have relationships with adults and peers around those interests and where they make a commitment to practice. Opportunities to do this will be restricted or unavailable unless the New Measures are valid and reliable assessments of learning recognized widely by the education system and employers.

TGIF

Here's a quote from Steve Jobs, the college dropout who most in the Deeper Learning world would revere around his incredible life's work in design.

"When you're a carpenter making a beautiful chest of drawers, you're not going to use a piece of plywood on the back, even though it faces the wall and nobody will ever see it. You'll know it's there, so you're going to use a beautiful piece of wood on the back. For you to sleep well at night, the aesthetic, the quality has to be carried all the way through."

When informal learning meets the formal learning (i.e., when out of school meets inside of school), we get engaged, high-quality learning. We are looking ahead and hustling sideways. In an interview with professional drummer Adam Christgau (https:// craftsmanshipinitiative.org/craftsmanship-side-hustle/), he talks about his side-hustle[1] of carpentry. As I kept reading, I noticed how he built connections to drumming, his main work, with carpentry. Adam could feel the flaws in his wooden drumsticks. He could feel when they were warping and when they were about to break and crack. Does he bring this knowledge to carpentry from music? Of course. Making connections is very common with side-hustles.

In the Craftsmanship Initiative, there was an article about the side-hustle. For some of us there's nothing new here. Kind of old wine in new bottles but side-hustles are definitely something to think about not only, in terms of the future of work but also, the future of school and where side-hustles fit. How off to the side will the side-hustle be in the future? When do you shift gears from one type of work you like to another? This is why we ask about many interests, not just one interest. How long does it take to get really good at something? How much time can school devote to students getting good at more than one thing and count it, when most students must take all the same standard courses and where only a few get any kind of hustle out of school?

Leading the Way

Looking back we also see an important distinction between leaders and managers. The people who make a difference and who transform education are not managers. Leaders are also contributors and they know how to do the work. The way management has developed over the years, we often have people who are in charge without knowing how to do the work. Not always but often, these people get in the way of new ways, they remain stuck in "reform" when new forms are needed, and they are all about compliance and meeting prescribed standards so new measures either don't make sense or are a threat to them.

A childhood friend Elliot's is the owner of one of the most famous literary establishments in NYC and the world called KGB Bar (uKraine Gallery Bar). This bar is a unique experience. It is a one of a kind establishment with a comedy club, jazz club, theatre and bar where the most famous

---

[1] A side-hustle is work done in addition to your regular job to earn extra money, for example, playing a gig on weekends if you are working full-time in a grocery store.

authors in the world do readings. When I go see Denis in the bar, we discuss both education and the bar business among many other things. One night after listening to me talk about schools, he told me:

Listen El, people in the bar business often joke that if you are in compliance, you are out of business."

I didn't have to think very long to realize that this tongue-in-cheek remark has relevance for education. Strict compliance undermines New Forms, New Ways and New Measures. The difference between an established environment that allows innovation and one that looks to write you up is perhaps the difference between where we need to be and what we have in education.

New Measures, New Forms, New Ways as NEW are defined by emergence, muddling through, exploration, discovery and self-organizing. Once you are a manager and in strategic planning mode then you are in reform, not new form. Once you are managing to a set of outcomes and to standardization, eliminating uncertainty, you are in reform. Once you are enslaved to KPIs (key performance indicators) and not guided by KPIs you are in reform not new form. Once you are focused on "outcoming" and not "becoming" (where people can search for and find meaning), you are in reform, not new form. As Elliot's polymath magician buddy Mark Mitton always tells him, "Beware when ambiguity is reduced to certainty and the physical is reduced to the mental."

The problem with reform is that people try to find golden algorithms, set patterns to fit people into; it is the standardization of standards and one size fits all. This is an All for One way to be smart without One for All ways to be smart. It creates misfits because the "how you are smart" is not counted, only "how smart you are" to a prescribed school standard. These are straightjackets that are hijacking youth for long hours in the day from finding meaning in their lives and instead teaching them how to conform. The big problem is you can't reduce ambiguity to certainty and school lives on certainty. Do educators truly believe that they can control not just time and content but the hearts and minds of our youth?

There is a reason why Wolf Blitzer calls his TV show the Situation Room. This is a term used by the military where everything depends on the situation, and the terrain is a refrain in the military. Contrary to popular belief, the soldiers on the ground may have lots of autonomy to execute on a plan where they are in the midst of the mire with their lives depending on it. This way of being and knowing follows more of an emergent, discovery, and exploration path, not a strategic plan. It is riddled with ambiguity and challenges. People vying for strategic plans are not on the ground. They manage the ground and as the song says, "a little learning is a dangerous thing."

We may need to point out that we are not against instruction, standards, strategy or certainty. Under the right conditions where youth are choosing and adults are guiding, facilitating and instructing all is good but, this is not the system we have. The new form is where the system, the institution moves more toward doing work not just within the school but out in the community. New Ways, New Forms, New Measures open the door where youth go out into the community. If they don't get out, it is because the system closes the door and has managed to keep them in. These New Forms open the door in our schools and youth development centers.

It is up to us to continue to learn how to live with ambiguity and uncertainty as we talk and walk WITH our youth and not let them put themselves in harm's way but rather create environments where there is the right amounts of challenge and support for doing authentic work. It is up to us to be mindful of how to develop New Ways where every student is the curriculum and the entire community is the school.

Avanti

In the next chapter, we present New Ways. These are New Ways that have been part of BPL for years, New Ways that we have developed from LTL, New Ways that have emerged from our practices, New Ways that have been developed by "muddling through and mingling with" or in response to needs and problems, and New Ways that generate New Forms and that require New Measures.

We do have to say that our New Ways are really not new. The thinking and practice of these New Ways have been around forever but what's new is the way and ways we are applying them inside and outside of the education system for each and every child. We see that the New Ways give rise and require New Forms, which likewise imply and need New Measures.

Chapter Two

New Ways

In this chapter, we want to explain the principles behind and the reasons for generating New Ways of doing things which provide the basis for New Forms and the New Measures that facilitate, recognize, and credit learning that happens in and out of school.

We will outline the key elements emerging as we muddle through our New Ways that help educators provide for equity in the learning opportunities and learning environments that they create for youth and students. We will show you how leaving to learn and RWL as New Ways form an essential part of the new. This chapter will set the stage for describing the New Forms of BPL which are the programs that have been devised and developed since LTL for bringing these New Ways into schools and in communities with youth whether they are in or outside of schools.

When we speak of New Ways, they aren't new, but we think that the way that we are bringing and applying them to education and learning is new. When we are talking about New Ways, we are referring to schools being *primarily* focused on learning rather than teaching; we are talking about Interests-Relationships-Practice being the focus upon which we design, construct and offer learning opportunities and support to youth and students inside and outside of school; we are talking about enabling, allowing, guiding, assessing and crediting young people for "how they are smart" rather than just "how smart they are" (in the first case, we honor a person's culture, competencies, intelligence and capabilities, in the latter, we honor content and limited standardized measures used for the purposes of comparing, sorting, and selecting young people). We are talking about off-track learning complementing (and often superseding) on-track learning; we are talking about, and we will need to explain these, "getting inside the outside", "with and want", "muddling through, mingling with, mattering to", "edge to center", tacit knowledge, fluid knowledge, and *real* real-world learning.

Learning or Teaching

Egyptian Caleb Gattegno, one of the most influential educators of the 20th century, believed there was a subordination of teaching to learning. His approach to education turned the traditional paradigm on its head when he recommended that teaching should adapt and respond to actual learning as it unfolds in real-time. McCandlish Phillips, writing in The New York Times (September 28, 1970), claimed that Gattegno, "does not therefore challenge American education on some point of methodology; he challenges it in the way Copernicus challenged the belief that the sun revolves around the earth - that is, at the heart of its most fundamental and most honored assumptions." Gattegno's words and insights remind us that for every statement in educational systems starting out with the phrase "know and be able to do" and not also "do and be able to know", we have lost the quality in learning and knowing.

It seems to us that if you think of nearly any school, at any level (K-College), anywhere in the world, you will find that they are designed primarily for teaching. Look, for example, at the architecture (corridors leading to classrooms, classrooms set up for a teacher to teach), the schedule and timetable (designed and refined for teaching), the formal curriculum (usually set up as separate subjects to enable teachers with specialized knowledge to cover specified content), the school rules (in place to make sure teaching can function in an orderly manner), and assessments (testing - mostly standardized - to ensure teachers are teaching and covering the content of the curriculum). Of course, any school is concerned with learning BUT they are primarily set up for teaching. And this matters as it creates the absurdity of a highly inefficient learning system even when one of its main tenets is striving for efficiency.

BPL schools, programs and assessments are designed primarily around learning. People don't just learn sitting quietly at a desk - we learn when we are walking, talking, playing, interacting, making things and breaking things, making mistakes and failing. We learn when all of our senses are engaged in school, out of school, in the park, at our part-time job, on the bus, in our room, at our grandmother's, in a garage, with our friends, through our interests, in relationships, when we are practicing - actually, we are learning all the time, everywhere. So, if we see the student as the curriculum and the community (or world) as the school, then our schools are going to look different, and so will our schedules, our exams, and the places where we are "allowed" to learn for credit and credentials.

In conventional schools, learners are often inhibited towards, if not deprived of, learning opportunities because of a well or over-organized program established by educators for teaching, where students have few or no decisions to make on a day-to-day basis. When people are told what, when, where, with whom, and how to do something, they may learn some content and gain a level of competency, mostly through memorization and repetition, but this is nothing compared to a learner making decisions about what, when, where, how and with whom to learn, most especially if it is connected with their interests and happening with others who share that interest and are willing to demonstrate their skills while allowing the learner to practice them. Of course, limiting and constraining what, when, where, how and with whom to learn stifles student agency. What turns information into knowledge that sticks is where there is agency, allowing us to pursue and practice our interests with others.

There was an increasing and well-founded skepticism even before Covid in the U.S. and in many European countries of the currency and value of a college degree. This has led (and has heightened as a consequence of families' experiences of school during the pandemic) to a questioning of the curriculum, role, purpose and practices of school, (high school in particular), which is primarily focused on teaching and preparing students for college. According to Philips and Jenkins (2018), "... the highest concern of families was this: Schools have a one-size-fits-all approach to teaching students, leaving behind those who are confused or struggling. ... Focus groups conducted with families around the country have found that ... families know exactly what their students need for an uncertain future: knowledge and skills. ... A similar project conducted by the Alliance for Excellent Education found, Students are not learning the knowledge and skills they need in the real world" (6-7). And, once again, the quality of learning is suffering because we are always putting knowing before doing and the abstract ahead of the concrete.

Interests-Relationships-Practice

One of the stand-out programs of BPL that will be described in detail in the next chapter is the Harbor Freight Fellows Initiative, which was designed around Interests-Relationships-Practice to enhance CTE, to highlight the rigor and vigor of the skilled trades to the public, and to identify and encourage youth with an interest in a skilled trade to participate in a 120 hour apprenticing experience connected to their interests. The lessons from Harbor Freight convey several insights gained through implementing the program - and these insights are not just relevant for CTE and the skilled trades but have implications for any educational program - and they are of even more relevance because most of the students involved as Harbor Freight Fellows are NOT in BPL schools but attend conventional high schools.

Stories of our Harbor Freight Fellows emphasize how youth operate in the world outside of school as they also receive instruction inside of school and how this can be brought inside of school then back out into the community as legitimate ways, forms and measures of learning. This is "getting inside the outside". We have been learning from Buckminster Fuller by **"doing less with more"** through our New Ways, New Forms and New Measures. Whatever level of restructuring or reforming educators might accomplish, it is likely to be built on a weak foundation because they are constantly reforming something that is not working. So, in that vein, let's not waste more time with reforms and let's get on with New Forms. And, once the new form replaces the old form, as Mae West, one of the many famous dropouts from Elliot's old high school, said, "Too much of a good thing ... is wonderful!".

That said, we realize that in a theoretical sense there is no such thing as starting from scratch. But also remember, you are not reading from a policymaker's perspective here. As practitioners, we are informed by evidence but our stuff is not based solely on evidence from research that mostly is done by isolating to a single variable. It would be wise for both policymakers and researchers to heed that message before they unscientifically objectify their findings as if those findings are without bias. As Yogi Berra used to say, "In theory, theory and practice are the same but in practice they are different." Call it what you like, our use of "emerging" and muddling through to get better at what we do is reserved for practitioners who can inform the field.

Therefore, it is much easier for us to start with more of a blank slate rather than patching up the existing system with its culture, structures, regulations and rules that, by definition, limit what you can do and usually stand in the way of the transformation that is needed.

How can we get students out of school and learning in the real world with mentors if we are tied to Carnegie Units and so many hours of "seat or instruction time"? Talk about agency. All this limits agency unless you break established rules and ignore the constraints of the system.

There may be some hesitations, cultural impediments, or restrictions in some schools or districts in relation to internships and leaving to learn opportunities being offered to all students, but there is no doubt that educators see the benefits. The chance for students to pursue their interests, practice and learn new skills, build relationships with adult mentors, search for meaning in their lives and expand their learning, career, and life opportunities is compelling. These opportunities create deeper and richer learning experiences where youth can explore and pursue their interests and engage in real-world practices guided by adult mentors who share their interests.

We have been asked many times and told that it is all fine a good to follow your interests but there are times, especially if you are poor or down and out, when you need to work to support yourself, your family, your children and you don't have a choice but to take any job - even one you don't like, so you can make ends meet or survive. This is especially the case if you are a woman, a person of color, someone with learning differences or gender preferences outside the norm that limits your options in the world we live in.

This is a very legitimate question. As a general response, what we do and what must be done with each and every student is to start at a young age when students and youth explore, figure out and try out what they are interested in with people and in places where that actual work is being done. Doing this at a young age affords the opportunities to find work that is entry-level around what you want to do, giving you skills and certifications that ensure you have things to fall back on that you like to do for a variety of reasons (i.e., what you're good at it, places and environments that treat you well, where you can make a living wage, the hours that suit you, and what gives your life meaning). Having these types of RWL experiences where you have built social capital at a young age is a way of hedging your bets about work in the future. Acting now when students are young instead of waiting for a time when you don't have the time, is the prevention to the question about living a life where you have limited your choices because you did not pay attention to this when you were younger. The more students we can have engaged in RWL, the sooner we solve these problems.

What if I don't have any interests? What if a student doesn't have any interests? Even after decades of speaking about Big Picture Learning and student interests, we never stop hearing this question. And, we never get undone by it. Although, some people ask it to undo us. Or, more likely, to avoid honestly rethinking their practice (if an educator) or considering if their child's education should mirror the one they had 30 years ago (if a parent).

Educators and parents both feel the need for change, but most are caught looking in the wrong places for answers. One place they rarely look is within children themselves. Adults often opt for telling, instead of asking, frequently letting their interests get in the way of finding out what the young person is actually interested in or what their needs are. They jump into problem-solving mode without the child's help. And, sometimes what they've identified as a problem is actually a child simply looking for an affirmation about how they're feeling. They just want someone to sit with that feeling with them.

Starting with the learner and their interests causes dynamic shifts in how we approach education and our engagement with students. When you start with interests, you don't know what a child is going to say, so you have to listen. This immediately changes the dynamic and the role of the teacher from one who knows content and answers to one who has to learn and find out. But, listening is not the only way we discover interests. Teachers need to observe students, and parents have to see what their children are doing. And, together, with the child, they need to design learning experiences that honor those interests.

When framed around interests, practice, and relationships, the benefits of leaving to learn are evident in the rich learning that happens when students leave school with a purpose. Students will encounter adults skilled in their interests, have opportunities to practice and develop new competencies, and they will experience new and interesting things. The research indicates that when this is the case (i.e., when students are pursuing their interests), this generates some of the best conditions for them to learn and benefit, to engage in exciting situated learning opportunities, and to develop autonomously. BPL and its programs are based on this well-developed theory of learning, and there is a large body of research as well as recognized best practices showing that student interest, serious and deep practice, and relationships with adults lead to high levels of learning (Bloom, 1985; Lave and Wenger, 1991; Deci and Ryan, 2008; Coyle, 2009; Blustein, 2011; Kenny, 2013; and Freeland-Fisher, 2017).

Here's a TGIF from Elliot that attests to the power of leaving to learn built around Interests-Relationships-Practice and demonstrates the tacit knowledge youth gain when they have opportunities to practice and learn the "tricks of the trade" with experienced and supportive adults.

 TGIF

Our Harbor Freight Fellows sessions at Summerfest featuring our Fellows Julie Torres, Fiona Nelson and Rakau "Rocky" Boikanyo were just amazing. We went from building Tiny Homes in Maryland to airplane maintenance in hangars in Vermont to a metal shop in Oakland. People stayed long after the sessions were over. Rocky's session included a live tour of the shop where he and his mentor Brian work. Rocky took out some of his metal art and a discussion ensued on where crafts, art and trades merge. In all of these conversations and demonstrations, it was apparent that our Harbor Freight Fellows' and mentors' use of language can only come from having done and knowing how to do work well. That's what tacit learning is and what schools need to be educated on, because in human development, grasping can precede and then forms language, but in schools that is rarely the case.

When Rocky talked about cold forging you knew he knew what he was talking about. There is a nuance and feel you get from someone who really knows. Another important point around how our education system is miseducating is when Brian Enright, Rocky's mentor, spoke so eloquently about being a mentor: "To be a mentor you want those you are teaching to become better than yourself." This is the difference between working for someone and working with someone, between teaching content and teaching a person. The system misses that one by a mile.

Off-track Learning

We wrote an article in Education Reimagined called "What are we losing by keeping learners on-track?", and we want to flesh out the importance of off-track learning as a new way. We argued that policymakers use big data to monitor student progress because they believe, as they always have, that by doing so, we can immediately identify who is on-track and who needs redirection, so everyone can graduate "on time." But, what does it mean to be on-track? What does a student know when they are on-track? Who knows they know what they know? What do we really know they know? And, when a student graduates "on time," what important things have we predicted in the process?

Policymakers and districts use graduating at 18 years old as an anchor because, from their vantage point, it is one of the only ways they can "easily" keep track. Therefore, "staying on-track" becomes an important phrase. This sounds simple to understand until you look at an individual person unattached to statistical averages. Once you do that, you have to know the student and where they are in many more ways than we currently take account of. Policymakers are placing a heavy bet that a narrow set of measures will suffice in determining whether or not a student is ready to graduate into a world where they will be measured by employers and their communities in ways far more complex than a simple score on a test.

Can we make off-track learning "legal"? When we were kids, the only betting that was legal took place at the racetrack. Of course, there were plenty of bets being made off-track (Scott's dad used to "run numbers", in other words take bets for a bar on the south-side of Chicago called The Sulky Inn). Rather than continue wasting resources cracking down on it, off-track betting was legalized. What was illegal became legal. Like betting, learning occurs off-track. And, like the betting days of old, only on-track (in school) learning counts. Off-track learning isn't illegal, but in the eyes of our education system, it's seen as second-rate or of no concern of the school and what students need to be achieving. In the world at-large, so much profound high-quality learning is happening off-track. To meet policymakers in the middle, why can't we use the same technology that tracks big data in the classroom to keep track of what students are learning in places beyond school - in the real world?

About a year ago, I was reading a story in *Craftsmanship Quarterly* featuring a high school student from Oakland (who we met above as a Harbor Freight Fellow). Rakau "Rocky" Boikanyo had been recognized as a Future Master for his abilities and skills. Rocky was shown displaying a prosthetic metal hand he had constructed in

two week's time. Is this student off-track? Does his unique creation of prosthetic hands count even though it's not part of any curriculum? Or, by doing what he loves, are he and students like him on-track? Can students get credit for being off-track from the standard measures? Are the schools adapting to the students or must it be the other way around?

At sixteen, guitarist and inventor of the multi-track Les Paul, another high school dropout, was asked by his mentor, Joe Wolverton, to join his band. Les Paul went home and told his mom,

I don't care about algebra and who sank the Titanic. Nothing means nothing to me, just Joe."

Was Les on-track or off-track? Why can't we have schools that allow students to leave the school building, engage in their communities, and credit their learning around their interests and what is meaningful and matters to them? Isn't this what micro-credentials are supposed to do?

Such stories aren't anomalies; they are completely natural. And, they shouldn't be ignored. By conventional school measures, Connecticut Congresswoman Jahana Hayes was way off-track. She left school to have a child, graduated from a high school that specifically served expectant mothers, took low-wage jobs, went to community college, and got a teaching job. While teaching, Jahana went on to graduate school and eventually became National Teacher of the Year.

Her story doesn't stop there. Twelve days before Connecticut's Congressional Democratic Primary, Hayes decided to run and came out victorious. She is the first African American woman ever elected by Connecticut voters to be in Congress. She is one of only a few black members of Congress serving a district where the majority of the voting population is white.

We are motivated to keep our kids in school, but what's the why behind it? To keep them on-track? What if Congresswoman Hayes never had the experiences she had? Would she have made history? Do we take the time to understand or evaluate our decisions differently for the benefit of the individual student? These are difficult questions to answer, but if we had a system that credited off-track learning, Hayes would be off the charts. What can we make of that?

How can we credit off-track learning? Perhaps you think there are great risks in trying to account for off-track learning. But, what if with the technology we have, we change our system so that every student had a learning plan whether they are on-track or off-track by conventional measures, and we manage learning longitudinally? At BPL, we have been advocating and using a personal learning plan for every student for decades.

We could consider all of these people with all of these stories off-track. Some graduated "on time," and some did not. Perhaps you are side-tracked or, like Les Paul, you are multi-tracking. Even when you are on-track, we are all always learning somewhere off-track. Hopefully, someday soon, our system will learn how to fit every student, to honor and count the many ways students really learn, and to make off-track learning "legal."

The combination of on-track and off-track learning relates to fluid intelligence - a new way of thinking about learning for many. Fluid intelligence is how you connect what you are doing to other things you start doing. This is Van Gogh's quote -

As you go deep you learn many things."

School is the antithesis of this by going a mile wide and only inch deep. Andrea Kuszewski (2011), amongst other researchers, points out that all of the following increase fluid intelligence - discovering new things, thinking creatively, challenging yourself, doing things the hard way, and networking and socializing. All five of these ways largely describe the "how" of BPL and the New Forms for doing that in our programs B-Unbound, Harbor Freight Fellows Initiative (HFFI), Los Angeles Leaves to Learn (LALtL) and Project InSight.

Tacit Knowledge

An interesting finding from the research that has been done on HFFI is the tacit knowledge that Fellows appear to have gained through their mentor and from practicing in a workplace. Tacit knowledge by definition is knowledge that is difficult to express or explain, and it is knowledge that one cannot get from books or simply from being taught. Such knowledge can only be obtained through actual engagement in specific activities in the context within which that knowledge is used and needed. Unlike school, classroom-based, online or simulated learning, RWL provides for the experiences from which real tacit knowledge can be acquired, practiced, embedded, improved and assessed. As renowned musician and teacher, Wynton Marsalis (2008) stated: "The best musicians know this music isn't about 'schools' at all. What is true about what musicians know is true in all fields and endeavors. Like my father says, 'There's only one school, the school of, "Can you play?" (51).

Induce, reduce, deduce, produce and all the other ...duces are more commonly used by us than educe. Most knowledge that people have is the knowledge they don't know they have. This is tacit knowledge, where you know more than you think you know or you know more than you can say. This is where you educe what is already there but has not yet appeared - this is the meaning of educate, "to lead out".

TGIF

The Nose Knows - Jimmy Durante -
"Your data sheet is not going to smell it."

This weekend, I got together with friends I have known since before we could talk. As it turned out, most everyone was interested in what I was up to but frankly, I thought what they were doing was just as interesting. Two of these friends were brothers, 14 months apart. One was a trauma surgeon at Daytona Hospital and now has a practice

working specifically on wounds that are hard to heal. The other went into commercial refrigeration and knows this work inside and out from fixing and repairing to the business. It appears that what they do for a living couldn't be further apart but what does this work have in common? What does healing wounds and fixing refrigerators and freezers have in common? It turns out quite a bit.

When I started talking to Steve about his medical practice and how he learned about trauma surgery and healing wounds, he revealed that he is a practitioner first and foremost. He's not a researcher or a policy maker and is proud that he has a practice. He's hands on. He told me that being a practitioner, "it is better to be thorough than brilliant" - a line I'm going to spend time thinking about. Interesting thing, when his brother Robbie overheard him talk about being thorough, he chimed in and agreed; the same is true in his line of work. But, that wasn't the big revelation. The big eye-opener came when Steve told me he smells the wounds as part of the diagnosis and treatments. Different infections smell differently. Once again Robbie chimed in, "I smell the oil from the compressor." They both agreed this important diagnosis is learned in the field, not in a book or classroom. You can't smell this stuff in a book. It takes time to get good at it and know what the smells mean and what to do next.

Working Nation and the Ad Council are doing a really nice job getting the word out in the media with a campaign to remove the "paper ceiling" that prevents people from advancing because they don't have degrees. Here we have an old issue for us - qualified but not certified. Until tacit knowledge is accepted and counted as a measure acknowledging you can do way more than you can say, the paper ceiling will remain.

Outside of school, you see tacit learning discussed all the time but without people using the term. When I picked up The New York Times, I read an article about Wille Nelson turning 90, "Willie Nelson's Long Encore". For lots of reasons, I've had an interest in Willie Nelson. One being a story written about him years ago pointing out how whether in his music or politics, he is always working at the edge but somehow resonates with the center. Most people trying to make change start in the middle and never get to the edge - the place of their vision - let alone appeal to such a huge cross-section of people who did not start out agreeing with them. Like Willie, at BPL, we aspire to be more edgy and resonate with the center. I believe this is how to bring changes we want to happen.

Edge to Center

As with so many stories of young people's potential being unlocked, it is often when they are exploring, adventuring, going out to the edges that they discover and find not only their interests but themselves and meaning in their lives.

 **TGIF**

A decades-old meme has been trending among educators - student-centered learning - also known as personalized learning, personalization, and students at the center; doubtlessly, there are other variations. I fear these terms have been captured and held hostage by educators hell-bent on transformation that simply replicate what they have already. It is not clear how a system based on rigid and narrow learning standards, testing and centralized systems

and structures can aspire to place students at the center. And so, the debasement of language so common in our society continues unabated.

*Anthropologist Tim Ingold (2022) advises: "As the criminal is sentenced in the court of law, so words are sentenced in the court of explication. Here in this court, academics are both judge and jury, both author and reviewers. Between them, they conspire to hold all words captive." Admonished by Ingold, and yet wishing to contribute to the discourse, I offer here an operational definition of "students at the center." It might be more accurate to say **student** at the center, since our BPL schools focus on helping each individual student -"One student at a time in a community of learners" - find their center, their stance, and their chosen pathways.*

The key for me is to help the learner find and explore their interests deeply, part of which involves exploring the edges of their interests and using that exploration to then "center" their own pathway. The process of centering includes getting edgy - pushing back the boundaries of what is taken for granted. Inspired by Jane Jacobs (1993), a genius in thinking about our cities, might we have every student declare their edge as their center?

A centering process involves helping the learner to explore many edges to expand the learner's vision and open up possibilities. Schools then help the student move between the center and these edges, often forming a new center. Schools can prepare the student to engage such center-to-edge, edge-to-center thinking and doing this as a lifelong learning process. The best

CTE programs and performance schools engage their students in such a process.

This work is guided by a strong evidence base but also by the observations of people who found their center - and keep rediscovering it - by going to the edge. Yo-Yo Ma reflects: **"There's a part of me that's always charging ahead. I'm the curious kid, always going to the edge."**

I find that we're good at talking about getting edgy, but too often it's only lip service. Once the rubber hits the road; namely, once students actually start showing their edginess, we pull them back. As Zat Rana points out in his article, **"Why Only Rebels Find Real Fulfillment" (2018, 18),** we tell students:

- **Don't be an artist because you will never make a living.**

- **Don't be an entrepreneur because you'll probably fail.**

- **Don't quit your job to travel because it's shortsighted.**

- Don't take the road less traveled because it's risky.

The world provides abundant examples of young people going to the edge and declaring it their center. In the civil rights movement, the Little Rock Nine did it. In the environmental movement and in the Women's movement, it was those youth who broke new ground, just as it was in sports. The X games, surfing, and snowboarding were all started by young people. Similarly, in math, science, and the performing arts, it is our youth and their adult trustees, coaches,

and teachers, who are with them to break through boundaries where they find their center at the edge. This navigation of student centering is not at all relegated to only the best in their field but to each and every young person wanting to do their best at the things they love to do.

Years ago, a friend, Herb Childress, wrote a wonderful ethnography that turned into a book titled, **Landscapes of Betrayal, Landscapes of Joy (2000).** Herb documented his observations of young people who attended a Northern California high school. He notes the happiness the students experience outside school, where they can be themselves and pursue their interests, and the unhappiness and boredom they experience in school. These students maintain a kind of equilibrium between the pull of the outside and the push from the inside that develops because inside and outside learning cannot be blended. There are many ways students get centered, but schools put students in situations where they can do little else but what schools want them to do. How edgy is that?

If we want to be student-centered, I suggest we start where students are meaningfully learning outside of school at the edges, mingling with people they want to learn from, inventing, discovering, creating, and seeking to understand. They go there to give their lives balance and find their center. They go to find the people and things that matter to them. It is then, as they "muddle through" and "mingle with", that our work with them as teachers and mentors and supportive adults emerges to guide, manage, facilitate, enrich, and instruct. It is often then that they feel that they "matter to" and that their interests, skills, abilities, competencies and learning matter.

Muddling Through-
Mingling With-
Mattering To

In LTL, we made lots of references to Seymour Sarason's use of the term productive learning, a phrase he coined that meant for teachers to start with what a student wants to learn - don't leave them there but start there. The key word here is WANT. To move forward from LTL we are now taking WANT (interests) and WITH (relationships) in combination, saying this makes for one of the most powerful learning environments there is and one that is attainable for all more easily outside of school than inside and facilitated by a teacher. With and Want together is a one-two punch where a student and a mentor share an interest and develop a relationship which in turn generates high levels of what researchers and educators alike refer to as social capital.

 **Livia**

From the moment she was born, Our daughter was filled with anxiety. She was hard wired that way. Livia came out of the womb crying, and didn't stop for years. It wasn't just from hunger, or being tired or needing to be changed, it was because of the strong footsteps and the loud voices of strangers. It was the bump in the road and the honk of a horn. Livia met all of her age related milestones, but it was a just a little harder for her because of that anxiety. She was the last kid in preschool to transition away from her parents and the first to run to us at the end of each day. As she got older, school never got much easier for her. She did well in her classes, but she didn't love being there.

The one thing that was constant in Livia's life was her love for the ocean. Since she was tiny, she loved everything associated with the sea - the animals, the fish, swimming, boogie boarding and surfing. Whenever she

was assigned to write an essay or do some sort of a project, she'd always try to weave in an ocean theme. As she got closer to high school, Livia was not excited to enter the 2,000 plus student filled high school we live near. It just so happened that a new project based learning high school had formed and Livia was thrilled to hear that it had an internship component. One day a week, students would leave campus to pursue an internship based on their own passions.

Livia knew exactly what she wanted. She had her sites set. When she started at the new high school, she went to work securing an internship. She made a cold call to the executive director of the Bay Foundation, she set up an interview and requested an internship. Livia was paired with Katie, a young new aquarist who was heading up a program to raise and repopulate abalone on the Palos Verdes peninsula. Our shy, anxious Livia suddenly loved Wednesdays. Livia came out of her shell with Katie, because they shared the same passion. Livia could actually spend a school day learning by doing activities that she loved. She learned so much about aquarium care, the abalone species, and participated in research projects. Her confidence began to soar and she became excited to talk to people about what she was doing. She was proud of her work at her internship.

The school's leaving to learn program has given so much to Livia. She has gained confidence in her academic abilities, in interacting with peers and adults, and it has given her a sense of pride. She now can't stop talking about college and where she wants to go. Who is this kid? Our shy, anxious daughter has truly come out of her shell. She has confidence in her goals for the future and is excited to pursue higher education.

Studies consistently elucidate the educational, economic and social benefits of internship and mentoring programs, and in recent years, research has become more nuanced to identify key variables or aspects of internships that generate the most benefit for learners. The research suggests that meaningful relationships are of most benefit to learners and indicates that relatedness is most likely to generate autonomous motivation in students. The newest research on this comes from a book, *The Good Life* (2023), the Harvard study which is the longest running longitudinal research of its kind.

The key finding about happiness and well-being has consistently been "having healthy relationships". This cuts across being rich or poor and across race, class and gender. So, why haven't schools paid attention to this data and made it a large part of their work? We feel everyone should, and although an obvious point, schools and colleges often overlook the fact that learning and interests become deepened through relationships with professionals in the community which in turn enhance life and employment skills. This happens because they are practicing and learning the "tricks of the trade" and receiving tacit knowledge in the relevant workplaces in relationship with adults who are working to real-world standards on interests which are shared.

The educational purpose of starting with interests is not singular. When you start with interests, you don't know what a child or student is going to say or where their conversation is going to go. This is muddling through and mingling with, but listening is not the only way we discover interests, we also observe. By watching, you learn.

 TGIF

It's not always what you ask, but where you ask a question, that matters. There is loads of research on situated learning showing that you will get a completely different answer depending on where you ask a question. Asking in a student's home, in a park, on the street, in an office or a classroom will conjure up all sorts of different answers or no response at all. Where you ask the question and what objects and people surround the student when you ask matters. This is why learning situated in a place of interest is so important.

It should be noted that interests are not careers and should not be used to direct students on specific pathways; instead, they should be harnessed as contexts for student learning. Most students in schools assume when an adult asks them what they are interested in, that the question is about what they want to be when they grow up. What we need to be asking is what students are interested in now. What do they want to get better at now, rather than what interest do they have that can be shaped into a career path. Asking for students' current interests is very different than inquiring about what job they want when they are older. We ask about and seek to discover student interests for a very different reason.

In schools, students are asked or given an interest inventory to place them on a pathway - "to put you in a box and sort you". When you ask, "What are you interested in now?" it is to engage them, to show that you are interested in what students are interested in and thereby develop a bond around interests. By asking what a student's interests are, you are saying, "I'm interested in you through your interest". This is powerful and goes a long way to create a bond because "if you are interested in what I'm interested in, you are interested in me. I feel my interests matter and that I matter". Now we are talking, and eventually we will get to interests that may lead to not one but many career options. "Students don't care what you know, until they know that you care."

I remember working with an advisor who felt she was stuck with one student, Chris, and just couldn't uncover what he was interested in. As it turned out, I was right there when the student came over to her before the start of the day and showed her a sculpture of a sneaker he had made. Chris was telegraphing one of his interests but the advisor missed it. We spoke about it and then off Chris went in pursuit of those interests. This is an example of observing; the advisor had been "listening" for Chris's interests but hadn't "seen" what they were. It is a learning journey not just a pathway to employment.

When Johnny started at a BPL school it appeared that his interest was being a bike technician. He did have an interest and already had lots of mechanical skills in bike technologies. Although he learned a great deal from his mentor that translated into academic skills and social-emotional learning, it wasn't until another year had passed that he took this ability to focus on procedures into the field of becoming an EMT (emergency medical technician) and then the next year a nurse. It wasn't the mechanical, procedural skills that were the real motivators. The reality was that it was Johnny's need to help people through the skills that he had. Johnny was all about caring for people. This was the interest he was pursuing. Unless you knew him and went on the journey with him, your guidance as an educator would have sent Johnny down a mechanical related pathway that was really not his interest. Mattering matters.

The Game Not the Score

Mae West who dropped out of Elliot's high school in Brooklyn, Erasmus Hall, is famous for saying: "The score never interested me, only the game." Schools should pay attention to this double entendre because we have a system that mostly pays attention to the score and not the game. Could it be that Mae West was onto something? Could it be that a key to engaging students in learning is to pay attention to the game and not so much the score?

"You're wasting your time!" - how many times have teachers and parents told us that? Whether it was comic books, sneakers, video games, motocross, skateboarding, yo-yos, rock 'n roll, hip-hop, graffiti and all of the accoutrements of clothing, coiffing and merchandising that align with these multi-billion dollar industries, schools told you that you were wasting your time.

Wasting time is precisely the point of play and gaming, but that doesn't mean that the learning may not be deep. The French intellectual Roger Caillois (1958), called play, "an occasion of pure waste: waste of time, energy, ingenuity, skill, and often of money." (But, he goes on to say), "Therein lies its utility, as a simulation that exists outside regular life" (6-7). Play is voluntary, not part of ordinary life, unserious, unproductive and uncertain. Bernie DeKoven (2013) in *The Well Played Game* states: "Play is the enactment of anything that is not for real. Play is intended to be without consequence. Play is for fun" (21).

It is fairly apparent that the difference between games and traditional academics taught in school is that the latter violates all of the rules of play. Precisely because school bills itself as serious and certain, it becomes the foil of gaming. In the hearts, hands and minds of students, it is often school and academics that become a pure waste of time and energy because school lacks what video and board gamers (and no doubt Mae West) refer to as the pull of the game and its environment where players share an emotional connection that allows the participants to go deeper and practice longer.

Over the years, through our practice, observations and research, we have come to find out that the engagement and learning in these games are something that educators have missed the boat on in developing meaningful ways to engage students in learning that is "deeper than you think." The deep construct, development and learning that ensue in games are things to admire and learn from not dismiss and condemn out of hand.

Could it be that gaming is tapping into something deeper within us about who we are and how we learn? The big question is: What can we learn that gaming is good at to keep students engaged and learners at the center? Let's take a quick look at what is often referred to as Deeper Learning. Here are the five components normally associated with Deeper Learning.

- **Mastering Core Academic Content -** (specified outcome)

- **Thinking Critically and Solving Complex Problems - (assessed primarily by prescribed examples and hypothetical situations)**

- **Working Collaboratively - (usually one grade given to a group for producing a result)**

- **Communicating Effectively -** (only through text and verbal)

- **Learning How to Learn -** (based on prescribed tasks)

- **Developing Academic Mindsets -** (specified outcome)

Schools tend to violate the principles of play and gaming and in many cases the principles of being learner-centered. First off there are pre-determined outcomes that are decided on by the school, not the students. These are Mastering Core Academic Content, Thinking Critically and Solving Complex Problems and Developing Academic Minds. Next, it appears that deeper learning is only about working collaboratively and not working alone. Gamers do both. There is a time to work/play alone and a time to be in a network that is chosen by the player. Then, there is an assumption about communication, so the outcomes measured by school are judged by a written test or a verbal performance. Games are much more visual, tactile and tacit. The inclusion of these senses opens up access to young people who use these skills to learn. Furthermore, there is an assumption by schools that children can't figure out how to learn and have to be instructed in learning how to learn. The opposite is observable almost immediately when children are gaming and learning naturally for that matter.

Here are a few more things that can easily be contrasted to school. While schools struggle mightily to engage students, gamers and players are engaged by the intentional pull of the game. While schools deal with set outcomes and narratives that have endings, play and games are frequently improvised and open-ended, and often controlled by the gamers. Schools are in charge of lessons and outcomes; gamers and players are in charge of making their own decisions in an in-the-moment environment - that's agency. Schools are certain. Games are uncertain, filled with surprise and mystery. Games engage a person deeply when they have just the right amount of challenge and repetition. So much of school has either too much repetition without challenge or too much challenge without repetition. The result is boredom or low self-esteem for many students.

In case you have an outdated notion of the skills people use in gaming, it is not merely simple hand-eye coordination, pushing a button to destroy an alien or asteroid. In addition to knowing and manipulating ergonomically and anthropometrically designed game controls with a multiplicity of functions, gamers normally have to create and operate a character, manage and address a series of interconnected short and long-term objectives, and engage in text or verbal chats simultaneous to playing and responding to emerging situations.

In its present form, most of online learning mimics school and not the deeper underpinnings of gaming. Worse yet, some educators think the trick is gamification; this misses the point. What on-line learning is hoping to accomplish is what some video and board games have done. Through play, gamers have figured out the right combinations of challenge and repetition; sharing and feeling; narrative and improvization; mystery and surprise; motivation and ownership. Significantly, all games involve interaction - with things, with people or both. Chris Crawford in *The Art of Computer Game Design* (1984) makes it clear that the crucial element to any game is interaction.

Thus far schools have consistently failed to do the combinations listed above with high percentages of students, and schools generally do not provide the crucial element of interaction to make learning meaningful. The sad fact of this is that school and its consequences are not a game - they have real meaning for fairness and equity in life, for young people, their families and our future. What can we learn from gaming and play to engage students? When players play the game, they are in charge of making decisions and dealing with the consequences in an in-the-moment environment. Are schools ready for the game or are they only interested in the score?

Avanti

All of these New Ways in one way or another come back to or connect with RWL, and RWL is where it's at. So much of school learning, the old and present ways, can feel fake, forced, unnecessary, pointless or "only for the test". So much of schooling is future oriented and concerned with preparation - preparation for the test, preparation for next year, preparation for high school, for college, for work, for life - but where is the relevance for "now"? "Children, we have to do this because you will need it when you get older". The answer to so many questions that students ask about school and the answer to why they are being asked to do things they don't like, aren't interested in, don't care about or are struggling to understand is ... "it might be on the test", "you need it to get good grades", "you'll use it one day" or "you will understand when you are older".

Often the best way that people "spot a fake" is through our senses, by feeling that it isn't real, "there's something not right about this". RWL is only real when it starts from students' interests, when those interests are cultivated and furthered in the real world with real people who are doing real work, and when youth can practice "those things" for real, right now.

We believe and we have learned since LTL that the New Ways that flow from RWL are the way forward. They lead to New Forms and they call for New Measures. In the next chapter, the New Forms of BPL will be presented. These are all new since LTL came out in 2013 and it is from these practices, from doing and playing, that we see the way forward for transforming education.

Chapter Three

New Forms

In the 1890s, office work was a new function that emerged from the industrial age and, architecturally, a new form was needed in the cities to follow and meet the needs of this new function. That form became known as the skyscraper and one of its pioneers was Louis Sullivan. It was Sullivan who coined the phrase "form follows function" in his essay "The Tall Office Building Artistically Considered" (1896).

Even though the impersonal nature of the industrial age certainly conflicts with our values, form following function is value neutral Sullivan (1896) was insightful and is often referred to as America's first truly modern architect. "It is the pervading law of all things organic and inorganic, of all things physical and metaphysical, of all things human, and all things super-human, of all true manifestations of the head, of the heart, of the soul, that the life is recognizable in its expression, that form ever follows function. It is the law" (408).

When Sullivan spoke of form following function, he meant that the exterior design of a skyscraper should follow, enable and reflect the interior functions. When we speak of form following function in the context of RWL, we mean that the exterior forms of learning (the programs and initiatives) should follow, reflect, enable and ebb and flow together with the New Ways (new functions) of learning to be activated. Therefore, in this chapter, we will present and describe four BPL programs initiated since LTL was written that embody, express and facilitate the New Ways we covered in Chapter Two.

Do and Be Able to Know

New Ways require New Forms to put them into practice, to set them within the learning journeys of our children, and to provide opportunities to sustain and scale them. In the last 10 years, BPL has created New Forms of RWL built on New Ways of understanding how best learning can be facilitated and harnessed. The New Ways have taken the Forms of a series of BPL programs that have been engaging youth inside and outside of school: B-Unbound, Harbor Freight Fellows Initiative, Project InSight, and Los Angeles

Leaves to Learn. These are the New Forms that we believe exemplify and embody the New Ways. They are New Forms, not RE-forms.

TGIF

*All of the small business owners we met with had great stories and their plans were life plans, not business plans. Their passions and interests were their driving forces. Their stories were rich because first they actually did what they did and then, could talk about it. Once again, this is akin to Bruner's **Acts of Meaning (1990)**. In one lunch I had with Jerome Bruner and (hand neurologist and author of* The Hand: How Its Use Shapes the Brain, Language, and Human Culture, *1998) Dr. Frank Wilson, we discussed how BPL's work is connected through the biological impulse to learn that includes doing something, then figuring out how to do it through trial and error that leads to a heuristic and rules and then, telling the story of what you did. For Frank and for Bruner (179), this expresses the constituents of narrative.*

- ***Agentivity (actions directed toward goals controlled by agents)** - You do something*

- ***establishes Sequentiality (change over time)** - You do it over and over (heuristics developed)*

- ***examines Canonicality (what is possible? real? acceptable variance?)** - You get rule of thumb*

- ***presents Personal Perspective (i.e., specifies a narrator)** - You talk about it over a coffee or a campfire.*

So, first you do something, then you talk about it. Then, there is a give and a take between doing and knowing, and knowing and doing. For most of the time students spend in school, schools have it the other way round and many times so do designers who are ideating first without experiencing (i.e., the mantra is "know and be able to do" and not "do and be able to know"), so they go from abstract to concrete and but not from concrete to abstract. Why is that? It's a great question with answers that have to do more with command and control and managing than educing, figuring things out and learning who you are. When managers and designers don't have "game" and think they can just pick it up because they are smart and empathetic - watch out!

New Forms Not RE-forms

Since the start of this millennium, most economically developed countries have been attempting to implement wide-ranging and sweeping educational reforms (by assuming they know what needs to be done and then telling educators what to do). In the past ten years, this trend has emerged in developing countries as well. Commenting on the initiatives taken in high income countries, the OECD (2006) concluded: "Although there was some real initial progress, these reforms have ultimately come up against a wall, or rather a ceiling, beyond which further progress seems impossible, leading increasing numbers of school administrators and educators to wonder whether schools do not need to be reformed but to be reinvented" (187-88). Could it be that we need to "do" first, then "tell", because we won't know until we "do"? Educational policy

makers and these educational reformers assume they know, so they "tell" educators to go and do. The process of exploring, discovering, muddling through and allowing New Ways, New Forms and New Measures to emerge is off the table.

Let's face it: Serious self-scrutiny has not been one of our notable characteristics. We are far more aware of what we want to change in others than we are of how we need to change. Salvation for our educational ills is only secondarily "out there." Primarily it will have to come from within an educational community willing to say that we have met the enemy and it is us."
Sarason 1990, 16

Our New Forms come from our practices (from our doing), and they are helping to transform schools and influence youth development organizations through experience; so, it is out of the doing that we know. Case in point, there has been a strong push for schools to change in order to provide students with what has been termed "21st Century Skills" or "21st Century Learning." In the last decade, numerous reports, white papers, and well organized and well-funded education initiatives have appeared with the express purpose to reconceptualize education for the 21st century. These initiatives have come to be known generically as 21st century teaching and learning (Note: not as learning and teaching). Some of these initiatives represent partnerships between school districts, government departments, and education ministries with large multinational corporations;

unfortunately, they are mostly old wine in old bottles. The process does not allow educators to do and learn what works; instead, like students, they are being told what to do, when, where and how - and then being inspected (tested) on whether they improved on standardized outcomes.

While diverse authors, reports, and agencies emphasize different skills, knowledge, and dispositions over others, the so-called 21st century skills have been expressed as the 4 C's - critical thinking, communication, collaboration, and creative problem solving. The literature suggests that there is an international consensus coalescing around the skills, competencies, and attributes it is believed young people will need to attain in order to meet the challenges of the world (haven't these skills always been needed to meet the challenges of the world?), but no one clarifies **HOW**, **WHERE** and **WITH WHOM** the learning of these is to be undertaken, facilitated and measured except by how we have always done this work. Again, we have the telling (and the assumed knowing) before the doing, so we end up measuring the same things we have always measured in the same places with the same old assessment tools, relying on the views of the same people.

Voogt and Roblin (2010, 2012), Scott (2015) and Chalkiadaki (2018) have demonstrated that there is a broad range of different attributes, competencies and skills that represent 21st century skills, **but there is little substantial evidence available on the most effective approaches to deliver those skills and where and with whom they should be delivered.** The conclusion of most commentators is that there is a disconnect between particular understandings of 21st century skills and their application.

This confusion or disconnect does not surprise us in the slightest because educational systems once again are attempting to apply a fairly unclear and ill-defined set of skills to an entire cohort or generation of **unique** students from many different backgrounds with tremendously diverse interests, skills, aspirations, resources, needs and passions. Then, systems are prescribing an in-school, mostly academic curriculum intended to teach these skills and competencies. The teaching is then followed by students individually having to demonstrate they have acquired these skills through traditional forms of assessment and testing, which, even if competency-based, are still testing the same academic skills usually in the same ways. And, the tests are always of an individual, not of a team or of collaborations.

It is little wonder why so many countries, despite commitments and even high levels of funding, fall short of transferring policy into practices and practices into positive transformations in the lives of students (Viennet and Pont 2017, Schweisfurth 2020 and Jukes et. al. 2021). We have to repeat what Yogi Berra said, "In theory, theory and practice are the same but in practice they are different."

Even when project-based learning or deeper learning is used in schools, the measurements and measures of the learning are not new. Here, academics are the coin of the realm and what is counted is academic credit. Are academics just academics or are they applied academics? This is a big question that relates to but is almost exclusively missing in the "teaching" of 21st century skills in schools.

We think that since LTL was released that we have developed the Forms from our practices that not only foster these 21st century skills, if you will, but go much further and deeper by enabling youth to explore their interests beyond the walls of the school with skilled adults that develop and achieve highly relevant competencies, build meaningful and opportunity-opening relationships, and credit that learning with authentic New Measures (see Chapter Four). We are always at a crossroads in our work. Do we go as we know, or do we know as we go? We make the road by walking - form follows function.

B-Unbound

The following excerpt from a TGIF refers to the moment when years of BPL "doing" led to the emergence of "knowing" that a new form was needed - B-Unbound.

TGIF

Putting learners at the center and student-driven are two different things. For many years, we have talked about what it would be like to do Big Picture without having the trappings of school. What would it look like? Last week, we got the opportunity to build this from scratch. We received funds to start this work. Our name has changed from Outlearners to B-Unbound.

B-Unbound has been a long time coming. For well over a decade, a few of us at BPL have been trying to do something like

**BE YOU.
UNBOUND.**

REAL WORLD
YouTube · Podcasts
Social Media

**NAVIGATOR
COMMUNITY**
YouTube · Podcasts
Social Media

THE NAVIGATORS
Young people 14-24 who want
to explore interests and find
meaningful connections

**SUPPORTIVE ADULT
DATABASE**

ADULTS IN THE COMMUNITY
Businesses · Families · Non-Profits · Clubs · Orgs · Chambers of Commerce

B-Unbound and a big difference is now we have funding, a partnership with Straight Up Impact Films, and ImBlaze technology that makes the connections both locally and from afar to supportive adults. We are striving to make access to B-Unbound easy and elegant so that the most youth possible can experience it. It is then that the work really starts. Take a look at the draft graphic (opposite page) that tells the story.

B-Unbound was created to connect youth to supportive adults who share their interests and to build a community of peers learning to navigate their way together. It has now evolved into multigenerational networks of support around shared interests for both youth and adults. B-Unbound's unique programming is supported by its proprietary technology that monitors and manages community relationships. This technology is a BPL creation, known in BPL schools as ImBlaze.

ImBlaze was built to enable schools to curate a set of internships that students can search out and request to pursue around their interests. Schools are able to monitor the search process and then track internship attendance, support participation, provide feedback and help enable student success. For the New Forms that BPL has created, this technology platform is critical. It facilitates the smooth operating of leaving to learn and RWL and allows for youth-driven learning by providing a secure platform and database of options with mentors and supportive adults linked to student interests. This platform is used by all the BPL RWL programs - B-Unbound, the Harbor Freight Fellows Initiative, Project InSight, and Los Angeles Leaves to Learn.

Partnering with trusted community-based organizations, B-Unbound trains advisors (Co-Navigators) who can guide youth Navigators in using the B-Unbound platform to find Supportive Adults who share their interests. In addition, the Navigator Community offers peer-to-peer engagement and inspiration. B-Unbound encourages Navigators to "be unbound" in their interests and pursuits, to not be bound by their circumstances, other people's expectations or their past learning experiences, and to be unbound and unleashed in pursuing their interests actively with the support of adults who share those interests.

B-Unbound has developed to serve as an umbrella for all of the leaving to learn programs of BPL which include the Harbor Freight Fellows Initiative (HFFI), Project InSight, and Los Angeles Leaves to Learn (LALtL). Elliot, along with Pam Roy of Straight Up Impact and the Viktor Frankl Institute, Anthonette Peña, BPL Project Director of B-Unbound, David Berg, BPL Director of Digital Innovation, and others at BPL created B-Unbound and designed it from the New Ways that had given rise to the New Forms in BPL schools.

B-Unbound has no entry requirements and uses connections with schools and its community-based network of youth organizations to reach learners. B-Unbound is not school-based, so any young person can get involved whether they are in school or not and regardless of whether they have any connection to BPL. B-Unbound provides the organizational infrastructure and a secure digital learning community platform that is able to connect young people to RWL not only with those near to them but also with supportive adults anywhere in the world. For B-Unbound, the learner is the curriculum, and the community, other Navigators, and the adults they connect with are their "school."

TGIF

On Tuesday, I flew to Oakland where I met with Charlie Plant for a Harbor Freight Fellows working lunch meeting at our favorite Chinese Restaurant in the world on 10th and Webster called Shandong. I haven't been back since COVID but the owner, also named Charlie, recognized me and we all had a wonderful back and forth. This place definitely has a "je ne sais quoi." They make their knife cut noodles right at the front window the way it used to be with so many storefronts in Brooklyn. It didn't matter - tailoring, shoe repair, cooking, rolling cigars, jewelry and watch repair, wood working, painting, etc. - everyone was street facing. No farmer's market. Every day was farmer's market. This is where we used to watch people working for hours and how we learned and developed relationships with them that led to work. Now we have YouTube. Where is the Love? There are trade-offs. When you know the people and they live in your neighborhood and so many are invested, it makes a difference. Shades of B-Unbound and creating community and meaning.

Searching for Meaning

We share the view of psychiatrist, Holocaust survivor, and originator of Logotherapy Viktor Frankl that people are searching for meaning in their lives while they are looking for connection with others and with their world. Frankl believed that this search for meaning is a feature of everyone's life and is idiosyncratic. In other words, there is not a single answer to the question of the meaning of life; rather each person discovers what gives them meaning, and this will no doubt be based on their personal,

cultural, and historical context, their interests and abilities, who they are, and what gives them fulfillment. Therefore, educational programs should help to provide a process of discovery as each person pursues meaning as opposed to a standardized or prescribed set of activities with the same goals for every participant. Frankl sees the main purpose of education as developing within learners the ability to make decisions, to take responsibility for their learning and in so doing to become free to acquire the competencies that they need to be the person who they decide they want to be.

TGIF

*Two days ago, the new Kennedy Center Honorees in the Arts were chosen. Once again, I was reminded that our book, **Leaving to Learn**, starts out at this Kennedy Center gala because so many of the awardees did not make it through school. This year's Awardees were Berry Gordy (left high school), Joni Mitchell (barely finished high school and finished only a semester at college), Bette Midler (did three semesters at college) and Justino Diaz (went to a conservatory). Schools have a difficult time holding students who are the most talented and ready to show it. This is reason for Big Picture Schools and B-Unbound to engage through interests and meaning.*

B-Unbound works to create an environment for youth in community to pursue meaning and to be guided in what they are pulled towards; people are pushed by a purpose and pulled by meaning in their lives, and because purpose is subjective and meaning is individual and to be discovered, B-Unbound does not prescribe activities for Navigators. Instead, Co-Navigators and Supportive Adults assist young people in their search for meaning by starting with their interests and creating fertile environments for them to pursue them. B-Unbound works from the experience that young people will be most motivated and best served when they are pursuing their interests with Supportive Adults and mentors who can guide them as they explore those interests and practice skills associated with them. The following quotes from two Navigators express how B-Unbound is doing this.

I am a former delinquent; everything changed immediately when I got to know my mentor. I started sculpting with wood then changed to pouring metal. I built a furnace, met a blacksmith and just love it. I can teach it now and do so with grade school kids. It is therapeutic and I spend at least 10 hours a week in the shop."

Before I started this fellowship I did not know about the importance of the water district and the benefits that come from being an essential worker. It has inspired me to want to work hard and keep a community safe with safe drinking water. I was not very interested before, but now I'm pretty confident that this is what I want to pursue."

Although he was not a Navigator or connected to BPL, a story in The New York Times (December 26, 2022) about Francis Rosario captures much of what our B-Unbound program is all about - and Francis lives in Brooklyn, where Elliot is from. Francis dealt with so many of the issues our students face on their journey navigating the health, education, foster care, housing and human service systems. His story is an example

of the strength of Frankl's message about the push and pull of purpose and meaning and of how school can extinguish or kindle the biological impulse to learn.

When Francis Rosario was 20 years old, he was a masonry intern and got the job of restoring the 19th century geometric roof of the Cornelius Kingsland Garrison mausoleum in Brooklyn's Green-Wood Cemetery. Green-Wood is one of the most beautiful cemeteries in the country. The dome of the mausoleum was badly stained and its masonry was crumbling. To do the job right, Francis had to match the color and the decorative pattern so it would blend precisely into the original. His work ended up being exemplary.

Francis's internship was part of a preservation program at the cemetery organized with the Metropolitan Museum of Art (MET). Francis had always loved drawing and he also excelled in math; his dream was to become an engineer. In his first two years of high school, he was an honor student and did especially well in his math classes, but his family circumstances changed all that. First, he was sent to live with his father and then he was put into transitional housing before ending up with a foster family. As his situation worsened, he started missing classes and even failing a number of his subjects.

Francis persisted however and was able to graduate and even enroll in a college to do engineering. As often happens, college was not what he had anticipated, and his personal circumstances coupled with the cost of college becoming unaffordable compelled him to drop out. Left to his own devices, Francis tried to figure out his next step, so he started searching for opportunities that involved skills he had and things he enjoyed doing, like drawing and sculpting. He realized that masonry and conservation work might be a good fit, so he did some online courses. After looking for some work in this area, he decided to apply for the MET internship program in masonry. This led him to then join the career program at Green-Wood Cemetery. Here he could combine his art and science "chops" in ways where he could earn a great living and make his community a more beautiful place.

Through Brooklyn Community Services, Francis was able to get a subsidized apartment. He is now moving towards financial independence and he secured a masonry apprenticeship with the city. He credits much of his success to the support of his foster family when he needed it and the patience of his mentors. The work of B-Unbound and of BPL in general is to make sure loads of youth navigate their way to meaningful work without falling on hard concrete over and over again.

Similar to Francis Rosario's story, B-Unbound supports learners through quality relationships built around their interests which have powerful positive effects on them in a variety of personal, academic, and professional situations. B-Unbound innovates by creating places and networks where young people enhance their agency and build their personal and professional support networks. The community of B-Unbound creates a nexus where any young person with a dream of becoming an artist or architect, a poet or programmer, a sailor or surgeon, a technician or technologist, can go to get the advice, practical skills, and resources they need.

The experience of BPL and B-Unbound and the story of Francis Rosario show that students who are learning with mentors in real-world settings develop skills and relationships that carry them forward into further learning and relevant career opportunities. The relationships they form with mentors create a supportive connection which is often necessary to keep students interested so they can see the relevance of their work and the benefits of further learning. Here's what some Navigators have been saying about their experiences of internships and fellowships with B-Unbound.

My mentor introduced me to all types of hardworking people. There wasn't one person that didn't help me - they were not hesitant to show me the ropes and were patient with me if I had questions. The best thing about these people was they allowed me to pick their brains. They even explained and showed me other life lessons that had nothing to do with the work. I am truly thankful for everyone I met and everything they did for me."

The biggest skill that was built was teamwork and communication! Probably the most essential skill onboard a ship. Things are easier when you have a lot of people assisting you or you are assisting them. I love working with the people I work with and I learn new things every single time I go out to work."

Before my Fellowship I did not have a plan. I was worried about where I would end up, and what things I should try to get by. My fellowship has taught me ways to do what I love in a way that works best for me. I have met many inspiring people, I have learned from their stories, and I am taking advice as it comes."

The internship showed me the type of education I'd need in order to get into the trade by having someone in the trade explain it to me. We have frequent conversations about the industry, different opportunities, and how to get there. He is a direct source of knowledge because he is in the industry. It was like opening a door into my future dream career."

I have been introduced to many people and opportunities from my mentors. I currently have the opportunity to work for the company in the future and to possibly have some schooling paid for in order to continue my fascination with this profession."

The difference that makes the difference here with all of our New Forms is that these RWL opportunities come out of student interests and have a co-navigator/advisor/teacher as an intermediary where the intermediary knows both the youth and the adult (mentor) and makes sure that the practice and relationships are going well. Most other mentoring, work-based learning or RWL programs do the youth/adult connection without either the interests of the youth or another adult intermediary in the relationship.

Harbor Freight Fellows Initiative (HFFI)

HFFI was the first emergent new form of BPL after LTL was written, and it has paved the way for and demonstrated the success of RWL. In just over six years, HFFI has spread out into nearly 20 states and has had close to 500 Fellows complete their 120-hour apprenticing experience in a skilled trade, ranging from aviation and auto mechanics, to HVAC,

the maritime trades, welding and forestry. Recognizing the need to start early, HFFI now has an Explorers Program for the skilled trades that gets youth connected to mentors beginning in middle school.

HFFI has been made possible through the partnership between BPL and Harbor Freight Tools for Schools (harborfreighttoolsforschools. org). Tools for Schools is willing to do innovative things that impact the long-term and to focus on exploration, emergence and discovery rather than just a strategic plan. Such vision and commitment has enabled HFFI to develop and scale at pace. Even though HFFI is focused on CTE and the skilled trades, it was set up to eventually be a design for all students regardless of their interest or pathway. This has already happened and spread through Project InSight and LALtL, and it is a new form for RWL that can contribute to the greater educational world.

We recognized long ago the need for high school aged students with an interest in a skilled trade to have the opportunity and support (including financial support) to learn from professional mentors in real world settings. Charlie Plant, a former advisor and principal at BPL schools, had a long career as a skilled tradesperson and was of the same opinion. With Elliot, they started Harbor Freight Fellows. HFFI provides paid fellowship opportunities for youth and, by partnering with schools and tradespeople, HFFI enables students to develop competencies and relationship networks linked to their interests through apprenticing experiences, so that they are equipped with the skills needed for life after high school and in the workplace (Interests-Relationships-Practice). Furthermore, HFFI works to open up the skilled trades to women and students of color who disproportionately have not been given such opportunities because of biases and quotas around race and gender.

There is a pressing need to transform CTE in schools and within CTE to raise the value, status, and reputation of the skilled trades as excellent and sustainable career choices. This need is glaring when one looks at the stark shortage in skilled tradespeople and its massive impact on the economy. Educationally, it needs to be emphasized that the cognitive skills required in the trades are every bit as challenging as, and in many cases more so than, high school academic subjects. The problem solving, organization, systems thinking and creative analysis of a system's weaknesses, and all the interpersonal skills gained in the workplace environment, cannot be replicated in a classroom and are not developed within a school setting. The emphasis on REAL work in a REAL setting makes the difference.

HARBOR FREIGHT
FELLOWS

The push to get everybody into college, the devaluing of the skilled trades and other pathways over the years as a profession and career, and the perception that "working with your hands" doesn't take much intelligence, have all combined to help create the mess we're in. The graphs and quotes below show just how bad things have gotten and highlight the need to enhance the status of CTE and to provide for RWL.

Our country faces a critical shortage of skilled trades workers, now and for years into the future. Demand is high and growing for the electricians, carpenters, plumbers, and others who build, maintain, and repair the infrastructure that supports the entire

U.S. economy. But, due to an aging workforce and limited awareness of opportunities in the trades, the supply of workers trained for these jobs is simply not keeping pace. The gap is already slowing down projects, driving up consumer costs, and limiting the ability of American companies to adapt quickly to major changes brought on by new technology or regulations." Soricone 2020, 5

The National Association of Manufacturers warned in 2018 that 2.4 million manufacturing jobs could go unfilled over the next 10 years with an estimated loss of $2.5 trillion in GDP. Across the skilled trades, about 75% of the workers are people aged 45 or older, with about a third of all skilled tradespeople in these categories over the age of 55 (see page 61).

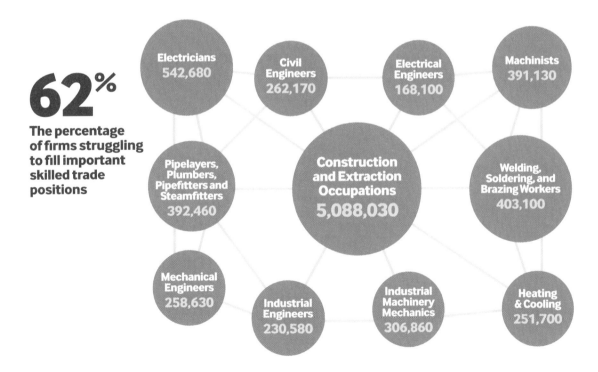

62%

The percentage of firms struggling to fill important skilled trade positions

Electricians 542,680
Civil Engineers 262,170
Electrical Engineers 168,100
Machinists 391,130
Pipelayers, Plumbers, Pipefitters and Steamfitters 392,460
Construction and Extraction Occupations 5,088,030
Welding, Soldering, and Brazing Workers 403,100
Mechanical Engineers 258,630
Industrial Engineers 230,580
Industrial Machinery Mechanics 306,860
Heating & Cooling 251,700

Source: adeccousa.com
The figures are the number of vacancies each trade had to fill in 2020.

The Oldest
Skilled Trade Jobs

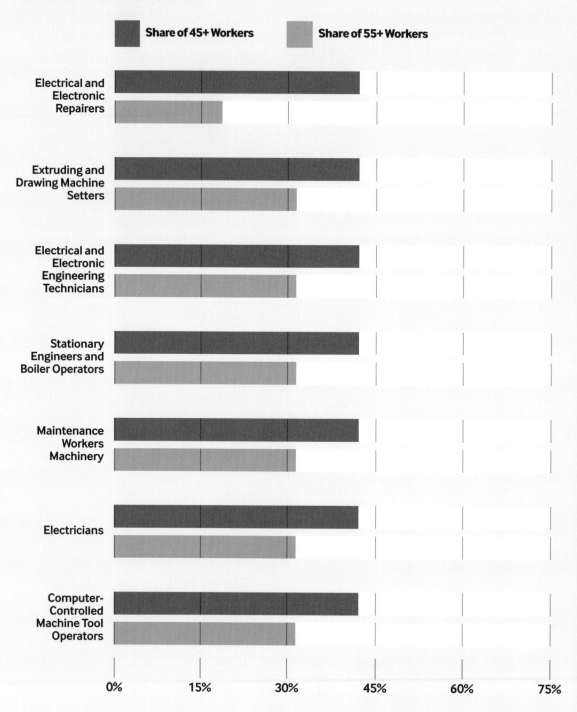

Share of 45+ Workers Share of 55+ Workers

- Electrical and Electronic Repairers
- Extruding and Drawing Machine Setters
- Electrical and Electronic Engineering Technicians
- Stationary Engineers and Boiler Operators
- Maintenance Workers Machinery
- Electricians
- Computer-Controlled Machine Tool Operators

0%   15%   30%   45%   60%   75%

Source: adeccousa.com

The United States is facing a perilous situation in relation to shortages and gaps in the skilled workforce. The data before COVID was showing that nearly two-thirds of firms are having difficulty in recruiting and finding skilled people. In 2021 that figure had risen to **68% with over one-third reporting that they are "slightly or extremely understaffed."** Over half of tradespeople (52%) say a lack of available workforce is stunting their growth and about 70% say they could grow their business if they could find more available workers (prnewswire.com). Millions of jobs are available and work needs to be done, but there are simply not the people out there, and young people, in general, are being discouraged in school from even considering the options of pursuing a skilled trade with the insistence that the only way to success is through a college education.

"On one side you have disengaged workers leaving their jobs and on the other you have skilled home tradespeople saying they are happy because they find meaning and value in their work, making it a unique and opportune time to attract new talent to these careers, while also improving employee engagement across the country," said Oisin Hanrahan, CEO at ANGI. "It's time to recognize that the skilled trades offer the opportunity for people to find engaging and high-paying careers. Everywhere there is a home, there is a network of small businesses that support that home and homeowner, and these are extremely needed and valued careers. Since the onset of the COVID-19 pandemic, there has been a steady increase in demand for home tradespeople ... yet, despite demand for the work and satisfaction among workers, the skilled trades have been experiencing a chronic labor shortage and, according to this year's report (2022), the perception among tradespeople is that the shortage continues to worsen" (angi.com/research).

 TGIF

My time at the Alexandria Seaport Foundation was well spent. Pam and I met with members of their staff and board around setting up B-Unbound as part of the next step in the evolution of their work. But, first off I want to note that their building is built right on the water and this in and of itself manifests the story of both changing climates and changing work. At our meeting, I finally got to meet Joe Youcha, past director of the Foundation. The next day Joe, Dennis Campbell and I had a long dinner discussion about the real skills that carpenters need to do their work enabling them to make high wages, benefits and pensions. All this adds up to work that has meaning and matters to society. It turns out there is way too much of what schools want everyone to know and way too little of what they need to do this quality work. The lack of attention by the system to each and every student's interests is devastating both morally and financially. So much of the system's standardized content is developed in the name of equity but with blinders on. There is a misunderstanding of just how intellectually rigorous, technically advanced and gratifying carpentry and other skilled trades are and how they are not dead-end jobs but actually lead to so many other careers.

From the sea to the air, the New Forms of B-Unbound and HFFI are having an impact. Beth White works with BPL and is an aviator. She has recently set up Habitat for Aviation whose mission is "To support the next generation of aviation maintenance technicians and avionics specialists for conventional and electric aircraft through apprenticeship opportunities anchored in relationships, relevance, and practice in an inclusive, welcoming environment where youth come to deeply know themselves and become deeply known by supportive adults."

Habitat for Aviation will be a B-Unbound Hub for Franklin County, Vermont furthering B-Unbound's mission to connect youth to supportive adults who share their interests and to build a community of youth learning to navigate their way together. Its vision is to develop and expand widely its first-in-the-world apprenticeship program for conventional and electric aircraft.

Along with HFFI and BPL, Habitat for Aviation is seeking to rescript the narrative around skilled trades and CTE as more than just a viable career pathway. It aims to serve as a proof point for learning through relationships, interest, and practice. We are using our New Measures (Chapter Four) of interests, practice and relationships to assess the fellowships and apprenticing experiences both in formative and summative ways. We are asking youth, mentors and educators whether interest and motivation are increasing - Are Fellows gaining practical skills that they can't learn from a textbook or classroom and, if so, what are they? Has a relationship been built between the young person and the mentor that will create further connections and social capital? Who knows that they know how to do something?

With the new form of HFFI, we are now moving this work beyond BPL into any schools or youth development organizations. To support and value RWL, we advocate for compensation to students in the form of a stipend and a stipend to teachers/advisors/Co-Navigators and mentors if they want it. All these programs are built on years of BPL experience developing Learning Through Interest in our schools.

Project InSight

Moving from the skilled trades, Elliot, Andrea Purcell and Carrie Ferguson discovered that there are similar needs and related opportunities in fields associated with eye care, eye health and working with people with visual impairments. With support from the Fox Family Foundation (foxgiving.org) and ASA, BPL established Project InSight which is based on the same ways and form as HFFI. Project InSight offers youth a 120-hour paid fellowship program with the triangular support of the Project director, mentor, and teacher/advisor. The main difference between Project InSight and HFFI is that Project InSight has to do preliminary work with young people to see if they have any interest in the fields of eye health, eye care, and working with people who have visual impairments. There was also an understanding of the inequities in health care and a sense that many youth who are furthest from opportunity are affected by preventable medical conditions, including issues related to vision.

For Project InSight, the level of work required to connect with and then provoke the interest of students is considerable, because eye health and vision care are areas and fields that most young people will be entirely unfamiliar with and are unlikely to have any connections or associations that they think of as a career. A further challenge is that Project InSight is working within a professional, medical field where internships for high school aged children are rare, equipment is highly technical, and links between schools and these professions are scarce. Moreover, Project InSight has worked primarily with under-resourced youth and youth of color; these are populations that are underrepresented in the fields of eye health and care. Impressively, all 35 of the Project InSight Fellows have been youth of color, the vast majority of whom are female. Rocio Rodriguez's story, in her own words, gives a great insight into Project InSight.

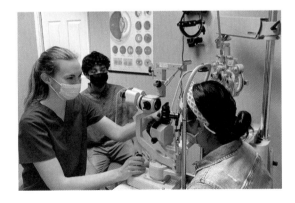

 Rocio

I've always known that my dream was to help others through medicine. But, as a sophomore in high school, being able to step into this field was extremely difficult. I was being turned away multiple times and not given a chance to demonstrate that I was genuinely interested in the field. Even though I was discouraged, I did not give up and kept searching for an opportunity. With the guidance and support from my advisors, I was offered an opportunity to participate in a Design Challenge to help visually impaired teenagers. Through this challenge, I developed an interest in ophthalmology. I wanted to learn more about eye anatomy, pathology, genetics and everything that was included in the ophthalmic field.

I shared my new interest with my mentors and weeks later, I was invited to participate in an Introduction to Ophthalmic Technology course. Throughout the course, I learned about the importance of technology in the medical field. Specifically in this class, it ranged from using tools to screen for visual acuity to operating machines to support medics in diagnosing patients. Personally, the most fascinating learning topics included pathology, diseases and conditions. This is where my interest in researching glaucoma began.

Learning about how common glaucoma was and that there was no cure or method to reverse the damage done, helped me realize that there are still many people who do not have resources for healthcare or an optometrist. This was when I knew that I wanted to take action and do something with regards to providing others with an opportunity to receive accessible healthcare. I was offered a chance to learn from a paediatric optometrist and work alongside Vision to Learn (visiontolearn. org) to provide school-aged children with free eye screenings and prescribed glasses. This was the most memorable moment from my mentorship journey. As I assisted the doctor, I felt as if I was actually making a change in other people's lives and within my community. Since then, the idea of becoming an ophthalmic paediatrician has been my dream.

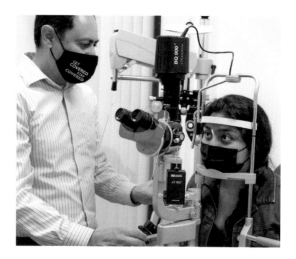

Project InSight gave me the opportunity to network with professionals and learn from mentors who are within my field of interest. From learning how to perform visual acuity screenings online to providing school-aged children with prescribed eyeglasses, I have been able to do what I love the most. Three years later, I am still very interested in medicine, research and working with children. As a college student at UC Merced, I am constantly using what I learned to seek new ways to get involved and new opportunities. Having mentors throughout my high school journey was life changing. I was guided every step of the way with my advisor and knew that if I ever needed anything, I could turn to them for advice. I learned the importance of perseverance, networking, and responsibility. I was able to learn lifelong skills, build relationships, and work on myself on a professional level. If it weren't for these experiences I would not be where I am today.

There's not much more to be said after that except that there is more to be said when you read the words of another Project InSight Fellow, Daniela Atenco Ortega.

Daniela

I think eyes are the most beautiful part of a person. It's the first thing you see when you meet someone for the first time. They can hold so much emotion and so much color. But I wasn't always interested in pursuing optometry. I did a couple of internships in my freshman and sophomore year of high school including a pet hotel and with an art teacher. I came to realize that although I loved doing these things, I didn't want to dedicate the rest of my life to them. In 11th grade I was a bit confused on where I wanted to intern and was having trouble thinking about future career paths I wanted to take. I began to think about my love for eyes and thought about what jobs related to them.

Since I had been wearing glasses for most of my life I started to wonder how all the machines doctors use would work and how they knew what to do with the results that came from said machines. I began my search for an internship with an eye doctor but I kept getting rejected from all the places I called, and one day one of my friends approached me saying she was in a program called Project InSight and thought the organizer might want to talk to me. I set up a meeting with the organizer to get interviewed and got in the program soon after. They were able to help me get in touch with a doctor named Dr. Wong who was searching for interns and I was able to get an internship with him.

I started going to his office for a couple hours each week and it was very difficult at first. I wasn't the type of person who liked to put myself out there or even interact with people. My mentor was very patient with me for which I'm very thankful for because it did take me a while to get the hang of things. However, once I got it I absolutely

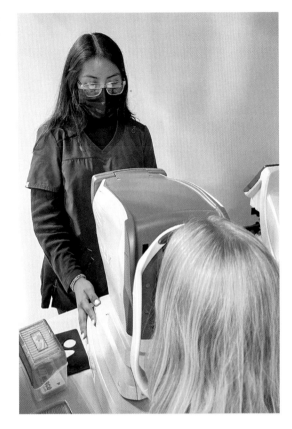

fell in love with the thought of becoming an optometrist. There wasn't a single day where I dreaded waking up early to go to my internship. But this internship wasn't the only thing I got involved with as a Fellow with Project InSight. I did many presentations with another Fellow and I even attended an eye fair at CSULA where I was able to give a speech about my experience. I'm glad I'm going to be able to go into college knowing what I want to study and having so much experience already. I'm the first person in my family to graduate high school and attend college so you can imagine just how excited and proud I'm feeling. I want to encourage others to also become a Fellow with Project InSight. They will not regret it.

Los Angeles Leaves to Learn (LALtL)

Inspired by *Leaving to Learn*, LALtL was set up in 2019, is directed by Andrea Purcell and is supported by ASA, the Leonard Hill Charitable Trust, and the Vera Campbell Foundation. The aim of LALtL is to enable the implementation of high-quality interest-driven career exploration through internships as a core component of schools and community-based youth and workforce development organizations across the Los Angeles region by providing the digital management system, ImBlaze. The initiative encourages and supports schools to make out-of-school learning a regular part of the educational system and school experience in Los Angeles County.

 TGIF

Moms as muses - **"Disinterest in school was a recurring theme that preceded "that talk" many rock moms had with their now-famous offspring to discuss dropping out of high school or college to pursue a career in music."**

Virginia Hanlon Grohl,
From Cradle to Stage, 2018, 45

For years, I have always thought about the parents of rock stars. What roles did they play in the lives of their children? What role did schools play with this cast of characters? David Grohl's mom Virginia has a new book out that probes these questions. She interviews the moms of Pharrell Williams,

Kelly Clarkson, Dr. Dre, Dave Mathews, Amy Winehouse and many others. All of these moms were very supportive parents and recognized their children's interests early on.

In Virginia's case even though she was a school teacher when David wanted to dropout, she thought it was the right thing to do and agreed. Most people/parents look at the data around dropping out and would not agree with her decision, but perhaps they are not looking in the right place for the measure that is important. Perhaps she is really not supporting dropping out but rather supporting her child's interests and choices that make lots of sense at the time. They are leaving to learn and dropping-in to explore their passions and what is giving their lives meaning.

Virginia states: **"Staying in school is one of the harder things musicians - and their mothers - have to deal with. School is very difficult. No one is assisting them in their love of this thing they're obsessed with. I could never make that different for him. And I was in the school. I was a part of that whole system. But it just - they had nothing for him"** *(47).*

The truth be told, none of these parents had a crystal ball. They did not know that their children would become famous. They did what they did because they observed their children doing what they loved and gave them what they wanted with guidance and love. What if their schools had provided REAL not FAKE support and engagement around their choices and interest? And, what if schools looked at the same measures around interests, practice and relationships that good parents look at. What's best for my child?

More than half of teens from underserved populations

believe their ideal education pathway would require less than four years to complete, and many feel comfortable following a different path.

Teens Want Efficient Pathways to Careers

55% said post-high school education should be less than four years

Teens Value Skill-Based Education

58% say a skill-based (e.g., trade skills, nursing, STEM, etc.) education makes sense in today's world

Because of the pandemic,

34% of teens feel more comfortable following a path other than four-year college

33% say post-high school education should only include subjects directly related to their program/major

Teens Want Their Education to Involve **Real-World Experiences**

 **7 in 10** say it's important to have internships/apprenticeships for their future career/job field in a post-high school education

Source: www.questionthequo.org

To achieve its aim, LALtL facilitates collaboration among educators to support students across geographic regions in Los Angeles in exploring their own interests with a view to grow and enhance access to internship opportunities for students connected to their area of interest. It may be considered ironic that after years of developing and offering school-based activities and programs in the United States "to keep kids off the streets", there is now a purposeful educational venture in California "to get kids on the streets" during and after school, so that they access opportunities to broaden and deepen their learning and to pursue their passions. The purpose of this is to encourage learning that not only builds on and extends what students learn in school but expands and develops their interests, provides new skills and competencies, and opens up all kinds of learning opportunities as well as important learning and life relationships for social capital and greater equity.

 TGIF

Alan Alda argues that the success of Scientific American Frontiers grew out of his realization that science, like everything else, requires a personal connection before any sort of understanding can be communicated between a mentor and a student. There is an episode in Donata Elschenbroich's film, Children and Soil, that quietly argues the same point. Middle schoolers in uniform are lined up for a lesson (i.e., didactics) on soil science. The teacher presents three different pots containing three different types of soil and then pours water into each, the object being to demonstrate the effect of soil density on the behavior of water in soil.

The narrator gently (masking the seriousness of the underlying critique) comments that most of the children can't even see what he is doing. The narrator also points out that in this school the teachers don't trust (hence, permit) the children to be in the garden with the plants so don't give them access to (let alone responsibility for) the garden itself. The result is bewilderment, detachment, and perpetuation of ignorance. He also makes the point that active participation (each one planting their own seeds) is essential for feeding each child's hunger for personal recognition.

Here's a quote from LTL saying the same type of thing.

Restrictions placed on youth while they are in school prevent them from having the productive learning experiences they crave. Students don't have enough opportunities of their own choosing in the daily school routine to pursue significant and enduring learning and to be treated as the young adults they will soon become. Lacking such opportunities, many young people do not sit still; they disengage, either psychologically or physically."

Washor and Mojkowski 2013, 20

The personal connection combined with doing things that matter out in the world are what matters. We have to allow children to learn the way we learn - by muddling through, mingling with, and mattering to. We often learn well by failing, by making mistakes, being given opportunities to "have a try"; this is practicing while being guided by people who share our interests and who care about us. Is there much scope in school to do this? Is policy advocating for these types of learning opportunities? Are youth able to leave to learn or are they forced to stay for standardization?

The research evaluation on LALtL found and highlighted some stories that really capture the benefits of leaving to learn. One student who exemplified this came from a school district where some time ago, a policy had been in place that students could not participate in an internship unless they maintained a certain Grade Point Average. This policy effectively excluded all the students in the Continuation School and a large number within the high schools that offered internships (Note: similar policies remain in place in many school districts not only in California but across the United States). Despite the policy, a student who had a low GPA was given permission to do an internship.

As a consequence of this one internship, the policy on GPA and internships was abolished across that entire school district for all students. The mentor of the student with the low GPA reported that he was the best high school intern he had ever had, even better than any college intern. This story highlights the power of internship experiences. In another school district, a superintendent said: "We had a low GPA student who interned in an attorney's office. When he finished that internship, he was on fire. Before then, it was iffy if he would graduate, but after his internship, he passed all his classes and did great; he surprised so many of his teachers." As one coordinator said, "Students with low GPAs tend to excel in internships; it's just a fact."

In one of the LALtL student surveys, the power of an internship is clearly in evidence.

I feel like I have become more responsible and can persevere. Since this internship, I have held myself accountable for my actions (going to class, my meetings, etc.), ensured that I understand and if not, ask for help until I do, and make sure that I am pushing and challenging myself - this is where the perseverance comes in. Doing the internships and taking this class online has personally taught me to not give up even if it is hard and seems impossible. It has made me more curious and always reminds me why I love doing what I'm doing."

From the school perspective, one principal contributed the following insightful observation.

At first, students don't trust it (exploring interests to do an internship). Many never had something like this. I watch students change. They go from not caring about their interest to being fully invested or importantly seeing that they are not interested in it. I see maturity. Kids are more focused on what really calls them; it's a beautiful process. Students now know what they want to do in college or in life because of internships. There's a big difference between "I don't know what I want to do" and "I want to be a nurse because …". I can't help but compare with a school I was in where there weren't any internships, and it's night and day."

These are powerful testimonies to the New Forms that have been initiated based on the New Ways. All these programs are RWL. It is fair to pose the question that we often ask of students - Is this real or is this fake? Here are the views of two mentors.

The real life experience is the key. They see consequences if they don't do their job or if they don't make it a priority. It's different when you are doing it in school where you can goof off and time isn't a real factor. We're doing this to make money, so speed and accuracy have to be right."

With the Fellowship, they learn to think on their feet. Like an athlete, they might know their x's and o's on the play sheet, but you have to adapt in the real world. The site is where preparation meets opportunity."

One Navigator who said, "It gave me real life experience that I can't get at any school or college" simultaneously captured the immense benefits of RWL having a mentor connected with one's interests and expressed succinctly the reason why transformation is needed and is overdue in school. The Fellow suggests that the knowledge and opportunities he gained cannot be gotten from a classroom or a book. The words of these Fellows testify to the difference that RWL can make to the lives of young people

I have wired up a few houses. I have learned every stage of wiring a house. Rough-in stage, and finish stage. I pulled lots of wire and made up lots of outlets. I learned how to put in switches and lighting fixtures. I also learned how to wire up an exterior panel."

I learned assembly of solar power cleaning robots, used many technical machines I wouldn't have been able to anywhere else, worked in groups towards larger projects with a deeper understanding of machines such as the mill."

My mentor would ask me to redo tasks that were not completed correctly or to the standards of the shop, and this helped me learn what I was specifically doing wrong and how to improve next time."

I look back at how I started and then reflect on it and I can see improvement in myself. I see growth in my maturity. I have become more mature and thoughtful. I have a different mindset and drive to work than I did before."

Avanti

The experience of learning first-hand from a skilled professional in the workplace is matchless and can never be replicated in a school. BPL has proven that these incredible learning opportunities can be made widely available to students and young people.

The challenge to the education system, however, is "does this new thing count? Will it be on the test? Can I use it to go to college, to get a job?". Often, if it's not measured, it does not matter. The next chapter presents the New Measures. Without these New Measures, most New Ways and New Forms will eventually fall by the wayside and end up like most well-intentioned, decently designed reforms - nowhere.

Chapter Four

New Measures

New Ways and New Forms require New Measures because you can't assess something accurately and reliably with instruments designed for something else; it's like measuring your height with a set of scales.

Standardized tests do not assess Interests-Relationships-Practice, for example, so we need measures that can account for a much wider range of competencies and abilities acquired through RWL, for off-track and out-of-school learning, for tacit knowledge and fluid intelligence, and for "how they are smart" rather than "how smart they are".

Years ago, Elliot and Charlie wrote an article called "No New Steps" referring to the movie *Strictly Ballroom,* in which a pair of young dancers exhibited their talent by taking their new steps out on the competitive ballroom floor. They gained the approval of a public audience, forcing the judges - who had earlier decided that there could be "no new steps" - into voting them the winners of the competition. One judge summarized their collective fears about changing the standards for ballroom dancing with the line, "If we let them change the steps then we're all out of a job."

The dancers would have never had a chance if they didn't boldly make their case publicly. They danced on their strengths and on their terms. They took dancing that was on the edge and worked it to the center. It is here that innovative practice turned into the accepted norm. Their new ways and new forms demanded and enacted new measures. After their performance ballroom dancing was never the same. In this case, the innovators understood the change by doing it, and then knowing, rather than by knowing, and then doing.

 **TGIF**

Andrew told me to listen to a program on ChatGPT and I did. It was a pretty wild program describing this breakthrough in artificial intelligence. The next day, we discussed ChatGPT at our Wednesday Meeting and had a great conversation about how our students demonstrate and exhibit what they know as a fail-safe way of making sure that what you say you can do, you can actually do. Given that ChatGPT is pretty damn good at instantaneously doing original papers and essays, solving math problems and who knows what else, what's a classroom teacher to do, or even worse a college professor, or worse yet some online college instructor who you "hand in" work to where there is very little connection or relationship?

Our work at BPL and with our RWL programs turns the tables on ChatGPT because you really have to show what you know, and your advisors and mentors know you over time. This is the "who knows you know what you know" of social capital. Now with Chatbots on the scene, policymakers will have a choice of tightening the screws to manage the way we continue to deliver content or paying attention to more competency-based ways of showing what you know. Ironically, these Chatbots can turn out to be the very thing that flips school systems toward a more human scale approach to learning, relationships, competencies, assessments, valuing communities of practice, and "doing before knowing."

"Is it live or is it Memorex?"

Here's the 1974 marketing from Memorex claiming you can't tell the difference between Ella Fitzgerald's tapes or live performances, but that just ain't so; of course you can. A recording is a recording - analog or digital. For thousands of years, marketers of the latest fads and technologies overpromise and try to convince us their product is amazing because they say it is, but is it so? Shades of Edward Bernays!

Will Chatbots deliver live or Memorex? Will these Chatbots change the glut of criminal and civil law cases and make algorithmic judgements that are fair and eliminate bias? Will they take the burden off of doctors swamped in a sea of medical data? Will they settle insurance claims fast? The list goes on and on. All of this is in our near future and has implications for places where we learn, and more importantly how we assess learning.

BPLiving

We will mostly discuss the assessment of learning in this chapter and the New Measures that BPL have developed over the past 10 years that support and provide for our New Ways and New Forms. We want to begin, however, with some important RWL measures (and the New Ways we have applied them) that affect everyone and that have a direct impact on learning, well-being, mental health and discovering meaning.

For years, BPL has been advocating for healthy living and preventative health measures to make sure students have the best chance possible to be well and to do well. On several occasions Elliot has been part of meetings at foundation, district and state levels where the sole focus was on improving test scores or increasing graduation rates through increased time for instruction, competency-based learning, project-based learning, design thinking and deeper learning. His suggestion, always ignored, was that if you simply want to see across-the-board improvement on these outcomes, all you have to do is make sure that students eat well (less processed foods and more plants and lower sugar, fat and salt intake), take regular exercise, have healthy relationships, manage stress, sleep well and avoid substances they have learned can be harmful to them. These are six lifestyle medicine measures and after writing LTL, Elliot struck up a relationship with the American College of Lifestyle Medicine (ACLM); subsequently, the six lifestyle medicine measures were introduced and implemented in BPL through BPLiving. Like the New Ways, the six lifestyle measures are not 'new' as measures of health and wellness, but they are new in how they are being applied and in the way they are used together by youth to promote health and address preventable illnesses.

Lifestyle Medicine Measures

BPLiving is an initiative that uses the six lifestyle medicine measures to foster and facilitate a culture of health, healthy living and healthy lifestyles. BPLiving is designed with, by and for youth to help prevent 90% of debilitating health conditions, to improve mental health, to enhance learning and the ability to learn, and to promote equity. BPLiving works in partnership with ACLM (lifestylemedicine.org) and FableVision (fablevisionstudios.com), a multimedia production studio, to promote its message and provide a first-of-its kind resource, offering a unique approach to health and well-being that originates from the meaning students find in these measures for their lives, their families and communities.

BPLiving is committed to developing ways that support youth, families, schools, and communities to take care of their health starting from their own interests in order to minimize pre-existing conditions. Youth connected with BPLiving have been creating, curating, and spreading health-promoting resources on the six health measures. Similar to campaigns to wear seat belts, to stop smoking and to stop drinking and driving, young people play a catalyst role in forming healthy attitudes, transforming lifestyles, and improving health in their schools, families, communities, and with younger children. We see our youth playing a similar role to youth in the civil rights movement of the 60's which brought change in society. The stories of two young people exemplify and testify to the power and impact youth can have.

Heidy

"Growing up in a predominantly low-income Latino community, I have first-hand accounts of how healthcare is considered a luxury, and those with vision impairments have a hard time receiving medical attention, medication, and equipment. The accessibility of health care my family and I receive is very little, due to our status and income, yet I have been extremely grateful for my ability to see without impairments, but because of my family history of developing obesity and type 2 diabetes at a young age, I am at a greater risk factor of diabetic retinopathy caused by type 2 diabetes. I have researched ways in which I can take preventive measures, such as lifestyle changes: exercising, and dietary changes. I have spoken with my family about public health, especially in Latino communities, by informing them about statistics on type 2 diabetes in Latino households and how we can take preventive measures to protect our eye health along with other systems in our body. I hope to create more community outreach on public health on eye care to ensure everyone can have a better quality of life."

Odilia

*"I reflected on the six measures and I was able to see where I was lacking and where my "**cups**"were filled. This practice made me more aware of my well-being. So often, I feel off mentally or physically and not know why or how to fix it. Now I am able to simply "scan" myself to see where I am lacking in my six measures and where change needs to be made. Mentally it's made me more relaxed in both my academic and personal life, because I feel fulfilled from working and, being aware of my lifestyle and well-being, I am able to focus on life's tasks such as school, work, and the enjoyment of life. I feel fulfilled and when I don't, I know what to turn to and how to fix and improve my well-being. A few tips on how to get started on a healthy life is to understand that it starts with you. What assisted me in becoming healthy was surrounding myself with others who are like-minded and have a goal of living a healthy life as well. Lastly, is to not be afraid to try new things and to be humble and moldable in order to absorb new information that can be applied to your life. I've been given more knowledge around health and wellness. The main change I've applied to my life is being aware of my six measures. Daily, I use positive affirmations, practice spirituality, deep breathing, physical exercise and being aware of my nutrition. What is included in my awareness of nutrition is to stay away from processed foods and eating more plant based with a goal of one day becoming vegan."*

Odilia DeGouveia is a graduate of the BPL MET High School. She connected with BPLiving through a course she was doing in College Unbound (collegeunbound.edu). She shared how she found ways to implement the six measures in her daily life. Heidy is a high school student in California who has been involved as a Fellow in Project InSight.

Schools across the country desperately need help in addressing students' overall development and well-being. Education and health professionals have historically been siloed in their practices - or limited by staffing constraints or available resources. "Without developing practical synergies, separate efforts have yet to solve the current gaps and to meet the increasing health needs that are set to worsen. The next generation most affected by the lack of support does not have adequate, culturally responsive resources to break this cycle." (UNESCO, *Futures of Education* 2021, 16).

By bringing together stakeholders from education, medicine, and public health to act collectively and prioritize the prevention of pre-existing health conditions, BPLiving is beginning to have an influence in addressing these issues that have a direct negative impact on the educational potential and the physical and mental health of America's youth. Too many young people, especially youth of color, have limited access to education around healthy lifestyles which jeopardizes not only their school success, but also their physical and mental health.

The health disparities in communities of color, due to marketing of processed foods, alcohol and tobacco, contribute heavily to an epidemic of obesity, diabetes, heart disease and cancer in much higher percentages than those of the general population. BPLiving is working with physicians like Dr. Marsha-Gail Davis of ACLM to decrease these disparities through prevention, using lifestyle medicine measures. This work is of great importance in view of what all the research is telling us. The statistics on obesity, for example, are reflective of why BPLiving and lifestyle medicine measures are needed.

The CDC (Center for Disease Control) findings on obesity in 2021 indicate the following. "From 1999-2000 through 2017-March 2020, US obesity prevalence increased from 30.5% to 41.9%. During the same time, the prevalence of severe obesity increased from 4.7% to 9.2%. (NHANES, 2021). Obesity-related conditions include heart disease, stroke, type 2 diabetes and certain types of cancer. These are among the leading causes of **preventable,** premature death" (cdc.gov/obesity/data/adult.html).

The National Library of Medicine comments on health disparities across the country. "The finding that minority and low income individuals are disproportionately affected by obesity is not surprising. The cheapest foods are those containing high levels of fat and sugar. Thus, the way to get the most calories for the least money is to eat a diet that is high in fat and sugar. This illustrates the interaction of biology and economics in supporting the obesity epidemic" (ncbi.nlm.nih.gov/pmc/articles/PMC3228640/).

Odilia and the high school students who are leading BPLiving are finding and showing ways to prevent and overcome the factors at the roots of the health epidemics affecting America's youth. Together they are inspiring others, including their families and communities, to view health differently and positively. As Odilia says, "My College Unbound project is to increase awareness and practice of self-care for low income parents through social media. I will apply the healthy living program into my career by applying any information learnt towards my clientele. I am currently working towards completing my certification as a Master Life Coach. Having learnt the importance of the six measures ... I could make a journal/log for my clients to utilize daily that would include the six measures."

Unless we attend to our own health and well-being needs, many advances we make in education will be of limited value or will be redundant if we succumb to preventable, life-changing illnesses. The New Measures promoted by BPLiving address this by starting with young people and facilitating them to be ambassadors and catalysts for transformation. The mission of BPLiving is to heal our communities with Health Equity through Lifestyle Medicine by delivering through these strategies. This is RWL.

- **Community Building:** To build a community that educates, empowers and encourages its members to obtain and sustain health equity within the underprivileged communities they serve.

- **Community Engagement and Empowerment:** To empower our communities to achieve true health through strategic and evidence-based community-engaged lifestyle medicine.

- **Community Partnership:** To engage key stakeholders in partnership and collective work to further efforts to impact our communities through lifestyle medicine.

> *If you take the "i" out of illness and replace it with "we", you get wellness."*
> *Malcolm X*

The International Big Picture Learning Credential (IBPLC)

The New Ways and New Forms we have developed in our schools and, more recently, in our programs will have very little impact on the educational system (and won't go anywhere) unless they can be measured and assessed. They will not amount to much nor lead to any transformation in education unless the assessment can stand up to scrutiny, demonstrate consistent validity, reliability and usefulness (for postsecondary education, apprenticeship programs and employers), and therefore, be widely, if not universally, recognized and accepted as a clear and trustworthy indication of a person's learning and competency.

We have good news - but first let's remember that current models of educational assessment shape and largely determine how schooling is structured and delivered, resulting in teachers prioritizing test results over learning, and channelling students towards limited academic achievements. As a consequence, the system undervalues and even ignores equally and more relevant competencies and cultural knowledge.

Way back in 1995 when BPL was started, Ernest Boyer, then president of the Carnegie Foundation, stated, "The time has come to bury the old Carnegie unit[2]; since the Foundation I now head created this unit of academic measure nearly a century ago, I feel authorized to declare it obsolete. Why? Because it has helped turn schooling into an exercise in trivial pursuit" (2). Nearly 30 years later, Boyer's critique of our standardized standards in "The Educated Person" (1995) still rings true. "Students get academic credit, but they fail to gain a coherent view of what they study. While curious young children still ask why things are, many older children only ask, 'Will this be on the test?'" (3). What does this tell us about what the education system values?

Education is one of the few fields, and perhaps the only system, that neither changes its standards nor the way it measures those standards as society transforms. The same old system of standards just gets more standardized. Outside of education, we often see industry standards change on an annual basis.

---

[2] In 1906, the Carnegie Unit began to be used to measure the amount of time a student studied a particular school subject. Typically in one high school year, if a subject was studied for 120 hours (about five 40 minute classes per week for 40 weeks), then a student earned one unit of credit.

An example is the health industry. In February 2018, The New York Times journalist, Anahad O'Connor wrote a piece, "The Key to Weight Loss Is Diet Quality, Not Quantity, a New Study Finds." Over the course of a year, two cohorts of people - totaling 609 participants - were either placed on a low-carb or a low-fat diet. The goal was to see which diet had a stronger impact on weight loss. Yet, even though both diets worked, the study published in the Journal of the American Medical Association (JAMA - jamanetwork.com), had an interesting finding: *"People who cut back on added sugar, refined grains and processed foods lost weight without worrying about counting calories or portion size."* With a single study, we can begin shifting our belief that weight loss is no longer about counting calories. Using the weight loss discovery as a parallel, wouldn't it be great if we counted less and started measuring more for quality in our students' work?

Sandra Milligan's 2020 research with colleagues, *Recognition of Learning Success for All,* demonstrates that, "Current forms of assessment privilege some forms of learning over others. ... Young people develop capabilities from diverse life experiences inside and outside of the classroom but because many of these capabilities are not measured or credentialed they are not recognised or visible to recruiters and employers" (4). The authors add: "We have found many instances of innovation. Yet much that is creative still sits at the periphery of education. New approaches need to be trialled and, if successful, scaled up" (7).

The long established one-size-fits-all method of assessment does not give a large cohort of students a full and fair depiction of their knowledge, competencies and abilities. As such, many students do not have the same opportunities as their peers, whatever their capabilities. Considerable talent is overlooked or lost with the impact weighing most heavily on the poorest and most marginalised youth. A standardized assessment system is most appropriate for a standardized learning experience which does not recognize the depth and complexity of a strength-based, culturally and personally relevant form of RWL.

The International Big Picture Learning Credential (IBPLC), on the other hand, recognizes the inherent value of all peoples so that youth are not excluded from further education and more desirable employment. The IBPLC allows for systemic change in schooling because teachers are allowed to facilitate and develop wider forms of learning, affording students more real-world and culturally-appropriate learning.

The IBPLC has its roots in the early days of BPL in the USA with its emphasis on "authentic assessment", the writing of ongoing narratives by advisors on each student, and the compilation of student work in portfolios. It took about 20 years, however, for the new ways of approaching assessment to be codified and developed by Viv White and her team into what is the IBPLC. The IBPLC originated with Big Picture Learning Australia and was developed through a partnership with the Assessment Research Centre (ARC) at the University of Melbourne, who warrant the credential through the RUBY psychometric assessment platform. The IBPLC has quickly become a proven, universally applicable assessment tool that provides for fair, culturally unbiased, school-based evaluations that lead to a stand-alone, digitized credential.

At the time of writing, over 1,000 students in the world have completed/are completing an IBPLC; most of them are Australian and there are some from Kenya and Barbados. This number will increase quickly because the IBPLC is now being piloted in the USA (in California, New York and Washington). Furthermore, the credential is already recognized by employers and industry. It is accepted for admissions consideration by half of Australia's universities and has been accepted by some colleges in the US, the Netherlands and Italy as well as the University of the West Indies.

*This week on a call with Linked Learning, they raised assessment issues we face in schools. How do you measure? What measures do you use? When do you measure? In some simplistic as well as in some complicated ways we have tackled this with ImBlaze when we get mentors to weigh-in in real-time at the workplace. The IBPLC has also gone further than anything I've seen to set real world standards with students driving the work. One of the many things I keep coming back to is that in order to assess well, **our assessments must be as high in quality as what we are assessing.** This is a difficult challenge.*

Person-Referenced

According to an Assessment Research Centre appraisal (2020), "The IBPLC presents a reliable picture of a student's abilities and competencies that can be used to determine the likelihood of success in postsecondary academic or workplace environments" (15). The IBPLC offers to ALL students, particularly those overlooked and undervalued by their educational systems, access to an equitable and educationally sound mode of assessment. "The IBPLC is a sophisticated tool representing a comprehensive certificate of achievement for students who are on pathways to college, employment, further training, or apprenticeships" (32).

Because the IBPLC is not norm-referenced, the credential avoids cultural, institutional and systemic biases in educational assessments, and it offers a reliable, viable, and scalable alternative to ACT/SATs and other standardized tools of assessment. Instead of assessments being norm-referenced, the IBPLC is "person-referenced" taking into account a range of experiences and evidence from school and out-of-school learning to establish discernible levels of competency.

Stewart and Haynes' 2016 study concluded: "We know that using standardized testing, a color-blind and meritocratic practice, as the de facto model of assessing scholastic aptitude and college preparedness has not benefited racially minoritized students. When used to assess accountability and college readiness, standardized testing undermines high-quality education, genuine student-teacher motivation, and the benefits of racial diversity, resulting in substantial inequities in college access among racially minoritized students" (124).

In November 2021 the University of California colleges announced that they had done away with SAT and ACT admissions tests. The UC President stated that they do not have an assessment that they can use effectively. Following this decision, they had their largest number of applications (up 16%) and enrolled their most diverse class of students, with the number of low-income students increasing by 10% (www.nytimes.com/2021/05/15/us/ SAT-scores-uc-university-of-california.html).

You could ask, as referenced above, when new, scientifically-backed information arrives in the health industry, why are they so willing to change their standards? Of course, the better question is, why does the education system remain so *unwilling* to change when study after study proves that many of our practices are no longer relevant? For example, despite the fact that only 19% of US workers report using basic algebra, we continue to use Algebra 2 as a gatekeeper for college admissions.

Not only in health, but also in many other professions and trades, increasingly more attention is being paid to ensuring quality and equity. This is having a direct impact on how they think about their own standards. Not long ago, The James Beard Award (which recognizes culinary professionals in the US) got ahead of the curve when they assessed contestants for, *the values of respect, transparency, diversity, sustainability and equality,* as well as taste and service. After they did this, guess what? The number of women and the overall diversity of people winning the award has dramatically increased, and the variety of foods and how they are served have changed significantly. They achieved equity through changing the standards, not by standardizing.

One of the significant problems with standardized testing is that by nature the tests are designed to be comparative and norm-referenced; therefore, they often measure the wrong competencies and only focus on content knowledge. Standardized tests primarily measure how students are performing in different schools by comparing students to one another, so the competencies that are being measured are very limited, and the priority is for results that allow for optimal ways to discriminate between students for comparison purposes. Standardized tests are simply unable to account for innate differences in students' abilities as well as in their socioeconomic background (Popham 1998, 2002; Kohn 2004, 2015).

Learning Frames-Portfolio-Video

For the IBPLC, six developmental learning progressions have been developed in detail, based on the six Big Picture Learning Goals that are in essence academics that can be applied in or out of school to assess and to support learning. Although our wording is different to capture these competencies and the way that academics are applied, they cover English, math, science, and social studies, as well as 21st century skills and those qualities and abilities that indicate "how you are smart."

- **Quantitative Reasoning**
- **Empirical Reasoning**
- **Knowing How to Learn**
- **Personal Qualities**
- **Communication**
- **Social Reasoning**

Each Progression is supported by an Assessment Frame, which is captured in the RUBY assessment instruments. RUBY is the on-line assessment platform designed and developed by ARC and informed by a decade of research. RUBY allows the assessment of complex competencies against developmental progressions and analyzes and validates the assessment data that are provided for each student. When the analysis is complete, a graphical indication of a student's level of competency is generated which is complemented by a student's online portfolio (which they curate) highlighting examples of their learning, work and experiences. The IBPLC also features a video statement produced by each student which presents their description of their learning journey, what they have achieved, and where they seek to progress. Importantly, the IBPLC allows students to stack credentials and certifications that they gain in and outside of school.

The assessment tool helps students to thrive because educators are not "teaching to the test" but are able to oversee, guide, and advise student learning, knowing that as students delve deeper into areas of interest and pursue those interests with mentors and through projects and work in and beyond the walls of the classroom, they are developing real world competencies and relevant skills which will be assessed against educationally sound learning frames and real world standards.

International Big Picture Learning Credential

Big Picture
LEARNING AUSTRALIA

THE UNIVERSITY OF
MELBOURNE

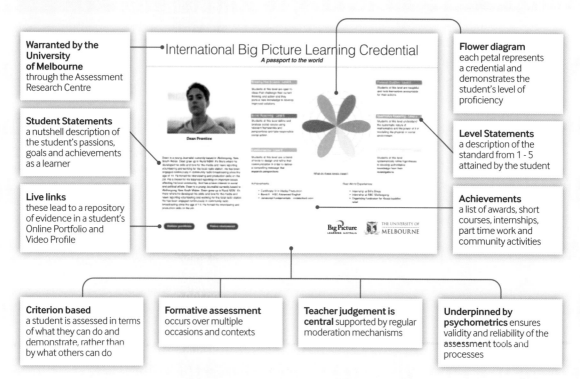

Warranted by the University of Melbourne through the Assessment Research Centre

Student Statements a nutshell description of the student's passions, goals and achievements as a learner

Live links these lead to a repository of evidence in a student's Online Portfolio and Video Profile

Flower diagram each petal represents a credential and demonstrates the student's level of proficiency

Level Statements a description of the standard from 1 - 5 attained by the student

Achievements a list of awards, short courses, internships, part time work and community activities

Criterion based a student is assessed in terms of what they can do and demonstrate, rather than by what others can do

Formative assessment occurs over multiple occasions and contexts

Teacher judgement is central supported by regular moderation mechanisms

Underpinned by psychometrics ensures validity and reliability of the assessment tools and processes

Families are delighted with the IBPLC experience and how it has positively impacted on their children's educational progress, college and employment potential, mental health, and self-esteem (Johnston and Milligan, 2020). The findings from the research and appraisal of the IBPLC attest to its functionality, usefulness, and scalability, stating that, "The IBPLC provides a reliable, accurate and rigorous measurement of the distinctive and valuable learning attainments of BPL graduates. It has the precision required for use in selection and recruitment of graduates into further study or work" (42).

ARC stated that it has no hesitation in endorsing the following views of the credential.

a **The profile and assessment have utility for learners and teachers to assist with developing learning agency, to plan future learning, and to navigate post-school pathways.**

b **The profile and assessments have utility for recruiters and selectors in postsecondary institutions and employers, to assist with candidates' selection.**

c **Universities are able to use the credential to differentiate between candidates reliably and validly for competitive courses.**

d **The way the credential is used for recruitment and selection is public, transparent, fair, equitable, and efficient. Attention was given to ensuring rigor and consistency in the assessment process.**

The scores and assessments generated by advisory teachers performed very creditably in the trials, with high levels of reliability and good performance on a range of psychometric indicators. No evidence of differential item functioning was detected. As stated in the report, "The level of performance of the assessments is very creditable, and moreover, it is likely to improve as the processes embed themselves over the years. The trials and pilot have demonstrated that assessment of this kind is able to meet the level of reliability and precision required of any high-stakes assessment. The use of the RUBY technology made collection of the judgements against indicators and quality criteria relatively straight forward, minimising the difficulties of managing such assessments across time, place and circumstance" (40).

The IBPLC offers a real unique and innovative form of assessment that can be scaled and which contains huge potential for cultivating, recognizing, and credentialling relevant and needed academic, vocational, creative, and sociocultural competencies. Remember, the IBPLC is more than just the Learning Progressions that are assessed from evidence using psychometrics. They are important but equally so is the video statement that is a central part of the credential and the portfolio that is selected by the students themselves to highlight their learning and competencies. The IBPLC is the intertwining of these measures, and it is this that allows the credential to show "how they are smart."

What is also so distinctive and meaningful about the IBPLC is that learning taking place beyond the walls of the school can be counted and credited. In what standardized test is a student's part-time job and the competencies they gain from it measured? How do schools measure the ability and learning of a young person who accompanies his grandmother to the doctor to translate and interpret for her? Does Rocky's prosthetic hand get measured on an SAT? What about Rocio's ability to perform eye tests? The IBPLC covers, acknowledges, assesses and credits all this learning.

If the IBPLC becomes firmly established and widely recognized as credible and useful for college and employment recruitment, a path opens up to improve, broaden and transform education away from narrower, more standardized forms of teaching and testing. The New Measures pave the way for the New Forms and the New Ways. Considerable work and funding will be required to transition the IBPLC to become authenticated and instituted in the USA, to be adapted for K-8 programs, and to become more truly international in its reach and reputation, but the pathway has been opened.

In our current education system, we act as historians and accountants - collecting and analyzing endless streams of data focused on a narrow vision that leaves little room for change - rather than being inventors and trendsetters. We can compare today's 12-year-old with one from 1919, but then again, after collecting over 100 years of homogenous data, what do we have to show for it? We can't expect to close equity gaps and provide higher quality education while relying on the system that created such gaps in the first place. As Mark Twain said, "Supposing is good but finding out is better." We need to

collect different and better data using different and better measures that look more broadly and deeply at each and every student. This data collection needs to be connected to teachers being allowed to use their judgement, skills, and experience. It can no longer be detached, impersonal, and imposed solely by distant assessors through standardized state exams.

Given that in so many other fields and professions there are new and different measures, we have to ask the question: Does our old data set and the way we collect the data prevent us from seeing the bigger picture? Or, is it something more intentional that maintains underlying biases and a status quo for only certain people? At the end of the day, our current system is set up to have a laser-like focus on standards that might not even be telling us what we most want to know about how our students are doing.

We might look at Ernest Boyer's (1995) closing words, "I hope deeply that in the century ahead students will be judged not by their performance on a single test but by the quality of their lives" (12). Boyer was asking the important question: "What, then, does it mean to be an educated person? It means developing one's own aptitudes and interests and discovering the diversity that makes us each unique. And, it means becoming permanently empowered with language proficiency, general knowledge, social confidence, and moral awareness in order to be economically and civically successful" (13). What standardized test measures this in our students? Shouldn't this be the standard of our school system?

CTE

As discussed in Chapter Three, the research and big data in industry are warning us that the United States is facing a genuine threat to its economy caused by the shortage in available skilled tradespeople and the undervaluing of CTE and a career in the trades. This situation is ironic when you consider the 2021 annual report from the researchers at ANGI showing that "Job satisfaction remains remarkably high, with 83% of tradespeople either somewhat or extremely satisfied in their choice of work" (angi.com/research/reports/skilled-trades/#ixzz7sfJWdQZB). Moreover, the most recent analysis by the Department of Data shows that occupations in the skilled trades are experienced as among the happiest, least stressful and most meaningful jobs in America. "Agriculture, logging and forestry have the highest levels of self-reported happiness - and lowest levels of self-reported stress - of any major industry category, according to our analysis of thousands of time journals from the Bureau of Labor Statistics' American Time Use Survey" *(Van Dam, 2023)*.

There has to be some explanation for the low reputation skilled trades have because, "The trades not only have a wide range of work options, higher than average salaries, and the opportunity for promotion and wage growth as older workers retire, but they also have a particularly compelling value proposition: tremendously high job satisfaction." Furthermore, research from ANGI shows that, "Looking at a topline analysis comparing a few well-known trades - plumbers, electricians, general contractors - average annual earnings are 22%, 29%, and 53% higher than that of the general population" (ANGI 2021, 12-13).

Some explanation can be found in the fact that since 1980, college enrollment has increased over 60%, (even though - wait for it - the costs of both two- and four-year programs have risen over 300% with student loan debt estimated to be 1.6 trillion). There is evidence that there are other factors at play. Most skilled trades are for, and are perceived to be for, white men. Then there's the perception that the economic benefits associated with the trades are not great and that the work is hard and doesn't take much intelligence or professional skill to join one of the occupations. These views are prevalent but unfounded.

These low expectations are cultural and are reinforced by schools. High schools do not offer many opportunities for students to practice and develop skills through RWL, especially in a skilled trade. The facilities, school schedule, and available materials are limited, even in CTE schools and Career Academies. There is little scope for students to participate in an apprenticing experience at a worksite with a mentor when they are in high school.

If students are serious about developing a skill, they have to practice outside of school, and such learning is not recognized or credited. In addition, schools tend to offer limited encouragement and incentives for students, especially girls, to pursue a skilled trade despite nearly every school district in America offering CTE. According to Gray and Lewis's survey for the National Center for Educational Statistics (2018), 98% of public school districts in the United States offer CTE in their high schools, but 42% of schools districts reported that one of the "barriers to student participation in CTE programs [was] teachers' or guidance counselors' negative perceptions of CTE" (32).

Research shows that many schools and teachers are communicating negatively to students about the skilled trades, including career counselors whose job is to give career advice and guidance. Schools are often devaluing CTE and the skilled trades. Soricone's (2020) nationwide research highlighted the need for significant efforts to be made to address this reality. "This was a consistent theme echoed by educators and administrators across nearly every state. Interviewees routinely reported that trades education is too often associated with "dirty" shop classes leading to 'dead-end' jobs. This misperception leads many students

and families to overlook opportunities in the trades" (8-9). She added: "The most common challenge facing skilled trades education - cited by nearly every state CTE leader we interviewed - is the widespread perception among students, parents, and even educators and school counselors that trades are a dead-end route. Trades education is often stigmatized as "just shop," a repository for low-performing students not expected to continue their education. This bias prevents many students and their families from understanding and pursuing opportunities the trades offer" (36).

Occupation Graphs

Key:  Women · White · Black or African American · Asian · Hispanic or Latino

Graph A

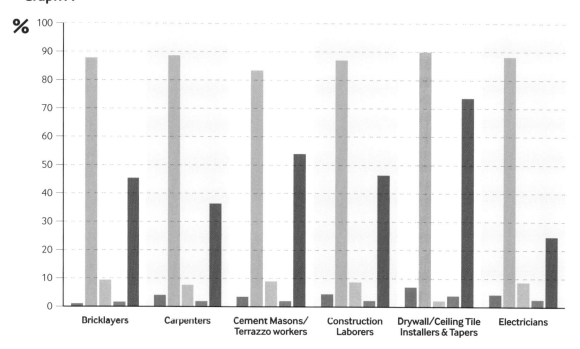

Graph B

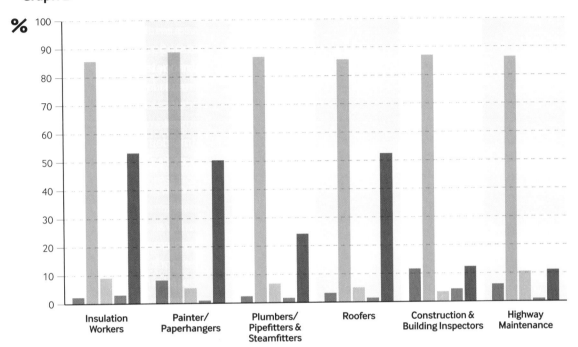

Graph C

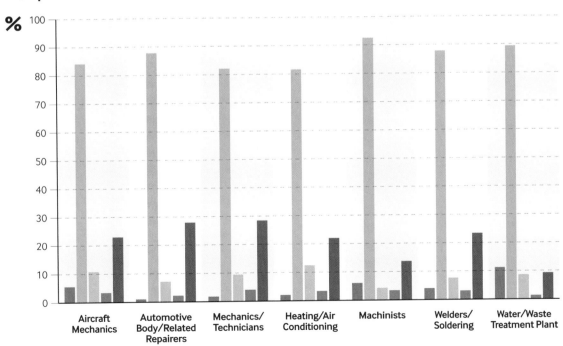

Source: U.S. Bureau of Labor Statistics 2020

Across the board, CTE and the skilled trades are not presented as desirable options for our children. The situation appears even worse when race, ethnicity and gender are considered in relation to CTE. African Americans are under-represented in all of the skilled trades categories, and, apart from automotive, manufacturing, and welding, Latinos are under-represented in all the other categories (ANGI, 2020). According to ANGI: "The skilled trades are overwhelmingly male. Electricians and plumbers are 98% male and construction supervisors are 97% male. The construction industry, which encompasses a range of occupations beyond just the skilled trades, is 89% male" (10). The 2020 US Bureau of Labor Statistics indicates that of all the Construction and Extraction Occupations in the United States, only 4% of the workforce are women.

Labor Force Statistics support the view that increasing the number of women and non-white people in the skilled trades would help to address shortages; however, for decades, education, labor unions and industry have struggled, and to a large extent failed, to create more effective pipelines to the building trades and maritime careers, especially for people of color and women. Are there barriers to these occupations that prevent, inhibit, or lessen the possibility of a woman or a person of color from accessing or even considering them?

The vast majority of skilled trade teachers are "white" and "male" with less than 20% female and under 15% teachers of color. The tiny percentages of women and people of color working in skilled trade occupations mean that mentor role models are even more scarce. A 2019 report, "Influences on Occupational Identities in Adolescence," shows:

> "
> *Exposure to role models, media, and instructional content influences how youth value and identify with different activities and occupations. Stereotypes create associations between occupations and identity categories such as race, class, and gender, creating barriers for many youth" (7). It's been found that participation in authentic communities of practice through work experiences, internships, and apprenticing experience have great significance on altering occupational identification."*
>
> *Callahan, et al. 2019, 1*

It is clearly important to have positive role models, especially educators and mentors with whom youth can identify and associate with as part of professions they are interested in. This is strongly the case in the skilled trades where ANGI reports that "Word-of-mouth recommendations continue to have an outsized presence as the preferred method of recruiting into the trades" (15). Word-of-mouth is the "who knows you know what you know", so transformation in the skilled trades can come through programs that focus on Interests-Relationships-Practice. In other words, when mentors in the industry have relationships with youth of color and females who are interested in a trade and can learn, practice, and demonstrate their skills, word will spread and perceptions and expectations will change. But, this requires New Ways, New Forms and New Measures because the old ways, forms and measures are most likely to continue to reproduce these inequities across industry.

311 Credential

As we said above, for many years the education system along with labor unions and industry have struggled and largely failed to create effective pipelines into building and maritime careers, especially for people of color and women. Over time, the unintended consequences of regulations and requirements by industry have distanced young people from the experiences and opportunities of working on-site.

Research demonstrates that on-site experiences and internships build necessary social capital and engagement where youth feel they can access positions in pre-apprenticeship and apprenticeship programs. The consequence of undue regulations is reducing the pipeline to a trickle, leaving out a great many youths who want access to the building trades and maritime careers. In response to this, we have created a way forward through New Measures activated in the 311 Credential.

The 311 Credential, along with HFFI, is part of this movement for educational change and for enhancing the status of skilled trades and maritime careers. Through nominations, the 311 Credential identifies students who display an active interest and a burgeoning aptitude in a trade and then offers them a pathway to develop and pursue their interest in a real-world work setting supported by practical and engaging classroom instruction. Like HFFI and Project InSight, the 311 Credential provides high school students across the United States with a $1,000 scholarship upon completion of a 120-hour apprenticing experience with a mentor connected to their particular interest in a skilled trade or maritime career (as well as a $500 stipend for a skilled trades mentor and $500 for a supporting staff member of a school/youth development organization or a B-Unbound Co-Navigator).

The Eastern Atlantic Regional Council of Carpenters (EASRCC) represents the Union of carpenters, cabinetmakers, floor layers, millwrights and piledrivers in Pennsylvania, New Jersey, Maryland, Delaware, Virginia, West Virginia, and several counties in North Carolina, as well as Puerto Rico. The EASRCC strives to promote job fairness and opportunities that provide family-sustaining wages and benefits. The EASRCC leads the way in training, educating, and representing the next generation of skilled construction professionals. The EASRCC places a top priority on developing the total professional: tradespeople who are not only technical experts in their craft, but who also demonstrate effective communication and leadership qualities. The EASRCC believes RWL advances leadership, skill, quality, productivity, safety, and attitude with the goal of creating a constructive culture within the construction industry and providing a competitive workforce. The 311 Credential is a solid step on the pathway to a Union career complementing EASRCC principles and priorities.

SkillSmart brings big data workplace expertise to the 311 certification. SkillSmart offers a comprehensive single platform (SkillSmart InSight) for capturing, storing and reporting on project, workforce, wage and business data, as well as a connected platform (SkillSmart Seeker) for community engagement around employment and building a workforce pipeline. This approach leverages the SkillSmart team's holistic approach to client success and ensures that goals are being met.

For the maritime trades, over 300 organizations that build and use small boats in their communities fall under the umbrella of the Teaching with Small Boats Alliance (TWSBA). These organizations annually serve approximately 100,000 youths and 100,000 adults. Many TWSBA groups focus on providing youth-focused workforce development through RWL. Such groups in Philadelphia and New Jersey are serving as both 311 Credential referral sources and as training sites.

The 311 Credential assesses RWL with New Measures that involve a partnership between mentors and educators. This allows Interests-Practice-Relationships as well as tacit knowledge and work-related competencies to be evaluated and credited. The name of the 311 Credential is derived from the way it is set up with its customized programs of RWL providing:

- **3 days with a contractor**
- **1 day certification training**
- **1 day volunteer activity with EASRCC**

Hence, a 311 Credential will provide pathways to postsecondary learning and employment careers. The goal of the initiative is to increase schools' and youth organizations' activity and capacity to place young people in professional RWL settings that are connected with their interests with a mentor who allows them to practice a trade. The initiative also aims to help young people develop relationships with adults in the field while gaining literacy and numeracy skills through the classroom practice in situated learning environments. The 311 Credential will get students out of the school and into their communities with the help of the digital platform ImBlaze which allows students to be tracked and connected with their instructors and mentors.

The 311 will not only transform students' learning but will also display its potential to provide meaning and purpose for their lives by developing intrinsic motivation and opening up a wide array of career and educational opportunities in the trades and maritime careers. We have already seen the difficulty that industry across America is having in recruiting and finding

skilled tradespeople. This is equally true for the maritime trades. Robert, 2018, states: "The Marine industry is rapidly growing, with new Marine jobs opening up all the time. However, there aren't enough skilled Marine engineers to keep up with this growth, leading to a prediction of a Marine skills shortage of over 300,000 seafarers by 2050" (2).

The stories of two Harbor Freight Fellows capture what the 311 Credential has the capacity to do. Maddie first discovered a passion for the maritime trades as a BPL student in Rhode Island, working on the Oliver Hazard Perry. "The first time on deck was amazing - I found beauty in the masts and the rigging, the wooden cap rails, the smooth, varnished helm. And then, below deck, I fell in love with the engine room, a metal jungle of pipes and valves. It's where the fun stuff happens. For my birthday, I got to take apart and clean a macerator pump! It smelled awful. It was great! My time on the Perry led to a greater interest in the maritime world, specifically in engineering."

Maddie was then extended an invitation to join a once-in-a-lifetime opportunity aboard Sailing Ships Maine's tall ship *Harvey Gamage* for the 2021 Spring Semester at Sea. Coming from a working-class, single-parent household in the inner city as a young woman of color, Maddie did not fit the typical sailor stereotype, but her will and determination were more than enough to make her a valued and respected member of the ship's crew. Here is an excerpt from her blog.

Maddie

In my last post, I described sailing as akin to a daydream. In this post, I'm going to talk about the less glamorous aspects of life at sea. But first, an update: I'm writing from Charleston, South Carolina. We sailed up from Saint Augustine, Florida, using the Gulf Stream to help push us along. And it was magical.

The water is as blue as lapis lazuli, clear as glass. We were around 80 nautical miles offshore one night when I had watch. Every star was visible; there were tens of thousands of glittering lights. I could even see the Milky Way! My amazing watch leader Rachel Young let us spend our watch exploring the night, finding constellations with a book and a laser pointer, stargazing, and appreciating the undiminished beauty of the offshore sky.

So, back to the nasty: Let's talk about the heads. For those of you who aren't nautical folks, "head" is the sailor's vernacular for bathroom. Here's how it works: you do your business, then you close the lid. You put your finger over an open hole on the wall, then pump a lever with your other hand. Toilet paper messes with the system, so that has to get thrown in the trash. I helped the engineer flood our blackwater tank (where all the waste goes), and we found a leak! It was a big one - the entire top of the plastic tank had come un-caulked, and that's why it smelled so terrible.

The experience of a different Fellow, Fiona, from Vermont, provides an insight into an exploration of the building trades and provides a fascinating reflection on learning. Fiona's piece highlights that the purpose of our work is on learning (not on final products) and is best judged from a longitudinal perspective.

 Fiona

Through Big Picture, I had the very real opportunity to pursue my passion of researching, planning, and saving funds for my tiny house project, while earning high school credit. I eagerly seized this moment and spent nearly three years devoting significant time to figuring out everything I could about building a tiny house. I knew this was a huge undertaking, but the complexity of this project suddenly became a lot more obvious when I had to arrange the transport and delivery of my new trailer. After six months and many rounds of negotiation, my trailer travelled across Pennsylvania and New York and was safely delivered to my

friend's backyard. Seeing the trailer sitting there was a huge relief. Reflecting on what I accomplished up to this point, I certainly knew far more than I did when I began this journey with Big Picture. I had been able to experiment, iterate, and push through failure.

At Big Picture, we follow the leaving to learn education philosophy - the belief that youth experience long-lasting, meaningful learning by accessing education opportunities beyond the four walls of our classrooms. This approach to learning reminds us of the great wealth of expertise that exists right in our own backyards, in the hands and hearts of our community members. When young people are in the real-world, working alongside mentors who are experts in our interests, we thrive.

To regain momentum behind my tiny house project, I realized I needed to find construction skill-building experiences that took me beyond my school building. As part of my research, I spoke to several architects and general contractors, but most were too busy to help. Thankfully, I connected with our local Habitat for Humanity and scheduled an interview with project manager, Chris Lane. Although Chris and his crew were toward the end of their building projects - focusing on flooring, painting, doors, cabinets, and other finishing details - it was still a perfect opportunity to get the hands-on experience I needed. Instead of sitting in a classroom daydreaming about tiny houses, I actually got to build one. How many young people can say that?

I reflect on the many things I am grateful for, and perhaps the biggest among them is the lifelong learner I've grown into who is steadily building a dream. The act of building with my own hands would provide me the opportunity to learn valuable skills that I will use for the rest of my life.

A "Hollywood ending" to Fiona's story would be a lovely photograph of the finished tiny house all done up and sitting pretty, but as we have stated several times in this book, life involves more uncertainty than certainty, and a happy-ever-after provides little in the way of learning. So here's the real story of how the tiny house ended up, captured in a email exchange with Scott.

Hello! Lovely to hear from you! A lot has happened in my life, but I'd love to help, unfortunately, the way my life has taken me means I never finished the tiny house. I worked quite hard on it and ended up getting to the point of it being framed up with windows, which made it look much more house like!

However, because of people I met online over the pandemic, I decided to go to school in England, which has been a great experience so far. I of course could not take the tiny house with me, and leaving it until I come back wasn't really an option since it's not completely weatherproofed.

This was a HUGE decision because as you know the tiny house was my passion project, and when everyone said it was too ambitious of a project, I said I would finish it even if it's just to prove them wrong. I then accidentally got emotionally invested in someone from another country ... which after a lot of consideration won out over my emotional investment in the tiny house. I'm now living with my partner in England and going to university. I ended up selling the house as a tiny house shell to someone equally as passionate about it, which was very important to me. This was by far the biggest and most impactful decision of my life as of yet.

So I'd love to talk about my experience as a Harbor Freight Fellow, and send you the most recent pictures, it just might not be the story you're going for. I've had a lot of talks with myself about the situation because to me it felt like giving up, but in reality I put so much time, effort, and money into the project and learned so much about both construction and myself. It was a very valuable experience and in a different life I would be putting the finishing touches on my house right now instead of writing a paper about confusing recycling symbols in the UK, but that wasn't the path I ended up going down.

I do however keep thinking "oh next time I'd do this differently" despite my focus for the next 4 years being school. I'm studying business, management, and accounting and hope to go into a career where I can move numbers around, but also use the project management skills I've acquired, and use the entrepreneurial spirit that got me building a house to take me wherever I want to be.

Thanks again for reaching out, let me know if you want to talk further or want pictures!

Hi Fiona,

Thanks so much for replying. What you have shared is really what it's all about. Our focus is on learning not completion of projects or never changing our minds and re-evaluating as we go along. It's actually a great story and although our time is tight to get the book to print, if you'd allow me to take what you've written, I think it might fit well in the chapter. I don't know if you know but I live in the UK (N. Ireland) - originally from Chicago. Thank you and let me know.

All the best,
Scott

The 311 Credential is part of the transformation of CTE, showing that a college education is not the only way to success and that the skilled trades and maritime careers should be held in high regard offering multiple ways for a challenging, fulfilling, and well-paid job. Based on the work of BPL, EARCC, SkillSmart and TWSBA, the 311 Credential provides a valid and reliable certification that meets its aims and objectives while opening up the pipeline for moving youth into the skilled trades and maritime careers. The 311 Credential has the principles, practices, and infrastructure to expand sustainably into more states and school districts while serving and inspiring an aspiring generation of students.

Avanti

The New Measures that have been presented in this chapter are for all learners and all types of learning. They are needed if the New Ways and New Forms are to be catalysts for transforming education, because they have to be accepted, recognized, and widely implemented to have a sustainable impact. Assessment of learning holds great power in the educational system and society because the results of assessments (test scores, grades) provide or deny access to postsecondary education, apprenticeship programs and employment. It won't matter much how educationally sound the New Ways are or how excellent the New Forms may be; if the learning can't be counted (assessed), it won't count.

We are dealing with big issues and endemic problems affecting our school system and influencing what happens in society. We have referred to the challenges of equity around race and gender, and it's clear that school success corresponds very closely to a person's socioeconomic background. So, a transformation in education is going to have many important implications beyond the confines of school. We are aware of this and think that a transformation is needed - not RE-forms but New Forms. And New Forms need New Measures.

The next and last chapter deals with policy, boring for many, yet it is critical for bringing about change and transforming education. We believe that practice in communities should inform policy and not the other way around and that these practices start in communities through RWL. The previous chapters have described our practice from our learning to leave. We contend that RWL and all that goes with it is the way forward.

Chapter Five

Looking Ahead

We want more and more students and youth OUT, because going OUT can change what happens going back IN. As we said at the start of this book, we wanted to get inside the outside, because that is where in these last 10 years we have found students and young people engaged, learning, discovering meaning, building networks of opportunity-opening relationships, improving equity and showing how they are smart.

For this to happen widely and fairly, we need to get young people outside of school at even younger ages and we need to be able to credit (and, where appropriate, compensate) learning that is happening beyond school. We also need measures of interests, practice and relationships with less time, focus and testing on traditional content, and more connections online where the student is the curriculum and the entire community is the school.

We have used the Italian word "avanti" to connect our chapters throughout this book. Avanti means "forward", "ahead", "let's go"; that is, "let us go", together, so we are moving WITH each other, and we are going forward towards the things we want to learn as a community of learners. We believe that when you do things with others, you learn, and, as you learn, if it is interesting, you want that learning to go somewhere. When you're excited about learning you want to use it and apply it, to help improve things, to figure more stuff out, to make new things, to work on problems that are difficult to solve or perhaps even unsolvable, and to help others. This gives lives meaning and purpose.

We are practitioners, not strategists - we do the work by muddling through together in communities, and then new work emerges. We are leaders and contributors, not managers. We believe that practice in community has to inform, guide, shape, and make policy, not just the other way around. We have always seen BPL as a part of a movement, not a model,

not a franchise, definitely not a project with a beginning-middle-end, and not just a group of schools. BPL is, and has been from the beginning, part of a movement to transform education and schooling through practice. Ten years after LTL and nearly 30 years since BPL started, we feel that we are in a place with our New Ways, Forms and Measures to continue that transformation at scale. This will involve funding and policy, and it will also involve community.

We are looking ahead with help from Julie Lammers of the American Student Assistance advocacy and policy arm. We are very fortunate to have ASA as a partner and are delighted that they have shared their policy pieces with us and allowed them to feature in this chapter. We have inserted our commentary (in green) about ASA policy around what Julie has shared with us (in blue) so we can show how our New Ways, Forms and Measures fit inside these policies and how our work helps to inform their development and affirm their value. Following Julie's contribution, we will set out where we see our practice leading in terms of educational policy, and we will look ahead to see where, over the next 10 years, our New Ways, Forms and Measures may go. We believe that the real policy question is about HUMAN scale with lots of self-organizing groups emerging from the community to get to scale. And, it will also involve communities sharing resources and supporting one another. How do we implement across the country so that as many students and youth as possible have real access to RWL?

American Student Assistance (ASA)

Allowing students to leave the classroom to learn has become more the norm at the collegiate level, but the concept has struggled to take hold in the middle and high school space. K-12 schools in the US have historically failed to think outside of the conventional box that learning can occur beyond the school brick and mortar building and past the hours of 8 am to 3 pm. ***Leaving to Learn*** described the shifts that schools would need to undertake to incorporate RWL into their regular programming, by "addressing student expectations for work in school, focusing on meaningful learning, and adopting New Ways, New Forms and New Measures". These changes are understandably daunting, but necessary if we are to ensure that every student in or outside of school has the skills necessary for the world of work.

Work-based learning in secondary education has made strides over the past decade, but wide participation in these opportunities nationwide still remains elusive. Expansion of work-based learning at the high school level is a policy priority for American Student Assistance (ASA) and we are pleased to collaborate with Big Picture Learning to ensure the right policies are in place to see expansion of these important programs. But we aren't there yet. A recent ASA study found that although 79% of high school students would be interested in a work-based learning experience, only 34% were aware of any opportunities for students their age[3] - and just 2% of students had completed one form of work-based learning, an internship, during high school.

In BPL schools 100% of students regularly participate in and complete RWL experiences connected to their interests, most of which are work-based with a mentor who knows them. Students' advisors serve as intermediaries supporting each student. We find that all our students are "interested in a real-world work-based experience," because it involves encountering adults who do the work they want to explore, learn more about and have a chance to practice. In addition to our schools, our New Forms (B-Unbound, HFFI, Project InSight, LALtL) facilitate RWL and work-based learning through our digital platform and with the guidance of Co-Navigators, Mentors and Supportive Adults. Furthermore, our New Measures (IBPLC, 311 Credential and BPLiving) credit this learning and create pathways for a much wider range of postsecondary options. Once again, this work is self-organizing and emanates from the student, where each student is the curriculum and the entire community is used as the school.

While the adoption of work-based learning by individual schools and districts is certainly crucial to its expansion, it is not the only lever. Policy, at the federal, state and local level, has an extremely important role to play in creating the right circumstances for the significant growth of leaving to learn programs. In fact, it is the combined effort of practitioners and policymakers that holds the most potential to lower barriers to work-based learning and make it a common practice in the middle and high school space.

Although most BPL schools are high schools, our middle schools and elementary schools also provide real-world opportunities and connections for career exploration. All of our New Forms offer middle school students chances to explore the world of work and a variety of professions.

[3] American Student Assistance. (March 2022) 'High School Work-based Learning: Best Practices Designed to Improve Career Readiness Outcomes for Today's Youth.' https://asa.org/wp-content/uploads/2023/01/ASA_WBLPlaybook_Final.pdf

In recent years, policymakers in several states, informed by the educators and employers on the ground who make leaving to learn possible each day, have enacted policies and practices to bring work-based learning to scale; expand its equitable access; infuse rigor, quality and accountability into its programming; and collect and use data for program improvement. We intend that the examples provided will help policymakers and practitioners alike, as they think about creating or increasing K-12 experiential learning opportunities in their own states and regions.

At the federal level, several major pieces of legislation, including the most recent authorization of the Strengthening Career and Technical Education for the 21st Century Act (Perkins V), the Workforce Innovation and Opportunity Act (WIOA), and the Every Student Succeeds Act (ESSA), have offered important incentives for states to create and strengthen work-based learning programs. For example, Perkins V funds can be used to support work-based learning in CTE programming; WIOA sets work-based learning as a required activity of Job Corps centers; and ESSA provides professional development for teachers and administrators on work-based learning instruction.

But to make high-quality work-based learning accessible to all students, state policymakers and education leaders will want to do more than what federal legislation allows. They must create robust offerings accessible through both career/technical and general education programming and develop student support structures, quality expectations, data collection processes, and program accountability mechanisms to ensure that all students have broad access.

We strongly agree that offerings must not be limited to CTE but also cover general education as well as other areas of life and work not covered by the school curriculum. All students benefit from RWL and work-based learning, especially when they are connected to their interests, create opportunities for mentor-student relationships, and give young people a chance to practice - to muddle through, make mistakes, and learn by doing - whether that is aviation or architecture, medicine or maritime trades, welding or wind farms.

In 2021, ASA and Bellwether Education Partners set out to understand states' approaches to work-based learning in high school. The research pointed to the eight most effective policies and/or practices to overcome common barriers to youth work-based learning. These eight are:

1   **Ensure Broad Eligibility and Widespread Equitable Access**

2   **Support Access for Underserved Students**

3   **Address Common Policy Barriers that Inhibit Expansion**

4   **Provide Financial Incentives to Encourage Employer Participation**

5   **Dedicate Federal and State Funding**

6   **Strengthen Statewide Infrastructure and Communications**

7   **Set Clear Quality and Accountability Expectations**

8   **Use Data to Drive Equity and Quality**

These common barriers are addressed and overcome with our New Ways, Forms and Measures. Everyone is eligible, the Forms are designed WITH underserved students not FOR them, most of the programs provide financial incentives that encourage employer participation, they have clear quality and accountability expectations, and they are based on solid research evidence that promotes equity and ensures quality through our New Measures. It is important that the entire community is involved in this process so that no one is left out.

Ensure Broad Eligibility and Widespread Equitable Access

Thirty-eight states have broad eligibility requirements for student participation in work-based learning opportunities in public high school and do not impose restrictions. However, some do set eligibility requirements that limit the number and type of students who can participate. Some states set age (typically 16+) or grade (typically 11th or 12th) requirements to ensure compliance with state labor laws. A more common way for states to restrict eligibility is by embedding work-based learning exclusively in CTE programming, or to make work-based learning opportunities available only in advanced level CTE courses that require students to have taken one or more prerequisite course.

Two states, **Delaware** and **New Mexico,** have two different approaches to this issue. These states either ensure that all students are eligible for CTE and thus for work-based learning or remove CTE requirements from work-based learning. **Delaware** requires all students to take at least three CTE courses in a pathway to graduate, and all **Delaware** students are eligible to participate in CTE. As a result, all students are eligible to participate in a work-based learning program. **New Mexico,** meanwhile, deliberately prioritizes

building work-based learning programs for all students, and not just CTE concentrators.

POLICY RECOMMENDATION: Leaving to learn is a way for students to connect real-world experiences to the classroom, and an opportunity for all students - whether their next step is college or career - to discover their passions, interests and career identity. These opportunities should not be restricted to CTE students, and states should create policy and programming that increases eligible access of work-based learning to all high school students.

We heartily agree. The last point is what we emphasize as one of the big benefits of RWL with the phrase, "who knows you know what you know", because that is what creates social capital. Furthermore, BPL has always had open access for all students with its programs. B-Unbound has no eligibility criteria and is open to all youth. The only requirement for HFFI and Project InSight is that Fellows are nominated by an educator who will act as an intermediary for their fellowship.

Support Access for Underserved Students

Creating broad eligibility and ensuring universal access to work-based learning opportunities is critical. However, states must also develop structures to target high-need students and ensure their success in a work-based learning experience. Very few states have developed explicit policies or programs to ensure access and success for underserved students. Less than half of U.S. states - just 19 - have developed policies or programs above and beyond the minimum federal requirements that are designed with the specific goal of ensuring high-need student groups can access and succeed in work-based learning opportunities.

Those states that do, such as **Georgia, Rhode Island,** and **Illinois,** take a variety of approaches to supporting underserved student groups, such as creating separate work-based learning programs for certain student groups (e.g., students with disabilities). Districts which apply to operate a work-based learning program must include details about the program's plan to support underserved students. These states also provide additional funding to ensure that students have the materials they need to be successful in work-based learning.

POLICY RECOMMENDATION: All students are entitled to high-quality leaving to learn programs, and in order to ensure that high-need students are accessing these opportunities, states must create explicit policies and programs to address the needs of underserved students whether that be disability accommodations, transportation to a job, special trainings and supports, or most importantly, access to paid opportunities.

Transportation is a big deal and needs to be budgeted for to provide access. If it is not, then a lot of students will be unintentionally excluded. We would add, as we mentioned in Chapter Four, that because many professions lack diversity (with women and people of color often greatly underrepresented), there is a need to pay attention to how this fact alone can serve as a barrier. If I don't see anyone like me in a particular occupation, it's clear that I may never even consider a job in that field as a possibility. This is why having intermediaries (such as our advisors, Co-navigators and mentors) can be so important in supporting youth to explore and gain experience in careers that they may feel excluded from or not see any role models who they can identify with.

Address Common Policy Barriers that Inhibit Expansion

There are many reasons to say "no" to starting or participating in a leaving to learn program. Schools and employers alike struggle with the logistics and scheduling of programs, management and staffing, workplace safety, liability, child labor laws, workers' compensation, and the costs associated with hiring a student.

Often, states fail to identify barriers because they are not collecting enough data on their work-based learning programs. This can make it difficult to identify trends in work-based learning participation and to understand how those trends might be driven by existing laws and policies that act as barriers to certain communities, districts, student groups, or employers. However, some states such as **New Jersey** and **Maryland** are actively working to identify obstacles and provide solutions. **Maryland,** for example, conducts regular surveys of students, employers and instructors to inform modification in work-based learning policy that can reduce barriers to participation.

Some states have enacted specific policies to minimize the reasons to say no to these programs. More than half of states provide stakeholders with a centralized work-based learning resource or manual that contains information and guidance about relevant laws and policies, and a handful of states have taken active steps to address known barriers, such as safety, liability, child labor laws, or workers' compensation.

Ohio, Connecticut, and **Delaware,** for example, have changed labor or insurance regulations at the state level to make work-based learning for younger students possible. **Georgia** passed legislation to help encourage employers to provide work-based learning experiences by changing workers' compensation regulations. And **South Carolina** has changed policy to address everything from scheduling conflicts between high schools and career centers to the expense of transportation for districts.

POLICY RECOMMENDATION: States must understand where current policy and regulations are creating obstacles to leaving to learn/work-based learning participation. This starts by collecting good and reliable data on the impact of policy. States then must work methodically to determine changes to regulation that will remove these barriers - do the labor laws, workers compensation regulations or insurance regulations need to be amended to allow greater employer participation? Do state laws encourage leaving to learn opportunities to be credit bearing and used toward graduation requirements? Are there state incentives in place to encourage employer participation or decrease the burden of transportation for districts?

We welcome what a number of states have done to open up more RWL possibilities to a much greater number of students. The challenge often comes back to the Carnegie Unit and the reluctance of schools and states to allow students out into the community and at workplaces during 'school hours.' It is therefore really important that relevant data is collected and that the measures used to evaluate the programs are in line with the desired outcomes (and 'becomes') rather than using standardized measures or

only viewing the benefits of RWL through a conventional school lens. The data also has to include the 'voices' of students as they assess their experiences of the programs.

Provide Financial Incentives to Encourage Employer Participation

Just over half of all states offer financial incentives like tax credits to offset high school work-based learning costs on the employer side and encourage businesses to partner with schools to offer work-based learning opportunities. However, these programs are often limited to employers offering certain types of work-based learning (most commonly apprenticeships), rather than being available to employers participating in all types of work-based learning. A few states, including **Delaware, New Jersey,** and **Vermont,** have programs that include a broader set of work-based learning experiences.

These incentives are most commonly in the form of tax credits for employers to take on a participant, as is the case in **Arkansas,** and with the School-to-Career-Investment Credit in **Colorado,** or the Job Mentorship Tax Credit in **New Mexico.** However, some states, like **New Jersey,** have created grant programs to incentivize employer participation. The NJ Career Accelerator Internship Program provides participating employers with up to 50% of wages paid to new interns, up to $3,000 per student.

POLICY RECOMMENDATION: A financial incentive to participate in work-based learning programs is an important carrot to reduce the financial burdens employers fear and which hold them back from taking on these programs. States should evaluate the kinds of incentive that would work best in their fiscal environment and consider a tax credit or grant program to encourage employer participation.

When we developed our New Forms, we recognized the importance financial incentives hold not only for student and employer participation but also for intermediaries who are the link in the relationships that ensure quality, accountability and safety as well as having oversight, which then leads to improvements, developments and expansion of programs. Additionally, the financial incentives raise the profile and status of the programs, recognize the value and real-world work that students do, and, in some cases, make the difference to whether a student can afford to participate in these programs or not.

Dedicate Federal and State Funding

The federal government provides dedicated funding for work-based learning at both the secondary and postsecondary level through the Carl D. Perkins Career and Technical Education Act (reauthorized as the Strengthening Career and Technical Education for the 21st Century Act, or Perkins V) and the Workforce Innovation and Opportunity Act. Under Perkins V, states receive block grants of funding that can be allocated to financially support all facets of CTE programs, of study and career pathways programs, including costs associated with work-based learning.

About half of all states also use grant funds or other time-bound sources of funding for work-based learning. While these programs can provide an important infusion of cash to support schools, districts, or other organizations to launch work-based learning programs, these funds are not a consistent source of support, meaning that districts and organizations may have difficulty sustaining work-based learning programs beyond the duration of the grant period.

A smaller handful of five states, including **Iowa, Massachusetts, Washington, Rhode Island,** and **South Carolina,** have taken the additional step of inserting a line item in the state budget or creating dedicated funding streams solely or primarily focused on creating and expanding work-based learning opportunities.

POLICY RECOMMENDATION: Nothing signals a state's commitment to a program like dedicated and sustained resources. States should prioritize dedicated state sources of funds to ensure the implementation and expansion of high quality leaving to learn programs.

Are the commitments states have made to these programs real or fake? Commitment is often spelled m-o-n-e-y, and the programs will not last or have much impact unless the other states take the step of inserting a line item in their budgets. It's like that quip on an egg and bacon breakfast about the hen and the pig - the hen is involved, the pig is committed.

Strengthen Statewide Infrastructure and Communications

Work-based learning infrastructure remains in the early stages in most states. Many states have adopted a "work-based learning coordinator" model and tasked those coordinators with communicating among stakeholders about work-based learning programs and opportunities. This approach to communications, though, relies heavily on the capacity and networks of a single person, rather than leveraging the collective capacity and networks of stakeholders statewide. Several states, such as **Nevada, North Carolina,** and **Rhode Island,** have also built websites to help match young people with work-based learning opportunities. The North Carolina Navigator, for example, is a free, first-of-its-kind tool where employers post work-based learning opportunities like job shadowing and internships, and educators search for, request, and track those resources in an open market environment.

An important infrastructure component of work-based learning is the development of an intermediary or public-private partnership. Because of the complexities of these programs, one thing that can be done to ensure seamless execution and simplicity for employers or schools is to have the coordination handled by a third-party. In **Washington,** for example, work-based learning is facilitated through a system of regional networks, intermediaries, and local coordinators that handle all issues, from scheduling to liability issues and pay. Similarly, **Delaware** and **Massachusetts** use community colleges and workforce boards to coordinate between local education agencies and business partners to implement and scale work-based learning activity. These coordinating entities take the burden off of local schools and employers to manage a program and allow for more seamless execution of program activities and data collection.

POLICY RECOMMENDATION: Statewide intermediaries can be an important component in ensuring that stakeholders have access to the information they need to develop, implement, and/or participate in high-quality work-based learning opportunities, and in communicating available opportunities to young people. Where possible, states should consider establishing an intermediate or coordinating entity to reduce the burden of participation for stakeholders participating in these programs.

We know that our New Forms could not function without our digital technology platform ImBlaze and the presence of our advisors, coordinators and Co-Navigators who serve as intermediaries. We cannot have New Ways, Forms and Measures without having some new roles, new technology and new networks and partnerships. We want to stress the importance of intermediaries who focus on relationships and actively connect students with mentors and other supportive adults. We should also note that our technology is designed for students and youth to search for work-based opportunities rather than it being designed for teachers searching on behalf of or for their students.

Set Clear Quality and Accountability Expectations

Although many work-based learning programs are developed and implemented at the local level, states have an important role to play in setting quality expectations and holding schools and employers accountable. States are at varying places in their development of quality expectations. Many states, including **Iowa, Georgia, New York,** and **Pennsylvania,** offer lists of roles and responsibilities for various parties, including the teacher or work-based learning coordinator, the employer partner, and the student, that can provide a framework for program design and establish expectations.

However, many states have not yet set clear quality and accountability expectations or developed systems to collect and use data on high school work-based learning for program improvement. An even smaller number of states have developed processes to hold either schools or employers accountable to quality expectations. Just six states, like **New York** and **Georgia,** have developed a quality framework and accompanying accountability for the school-based elements of a work-based learning program (e.g., standards for the instructor or coordinator, expectations about student evaluation, etc.); just one, **Washington,** has done so explicitly for worksite experiences (e.g., setting standards for what a quality worksite mentor looks like, etc.). In order to operate a Career Launch program in **Washington,** however, an employer must complete an application, undergo a rigorous review process, and receive an endorsement every three years.

POLICY RECOMMENDATION: States will want to do more to ensure they are setting clear quality and accountability standards for all participants in a work-based learning program so that everyone involved knows their responsibilities and can ensure the best possible outcomes for student participation. This might include a certification process for participation.

We certainly recognize the need for intermediaries and for quality, and we endorse accountability standards as long as they are real-world standards and not standardized, school-only standards. We think that employers have to be involved in quality assurance and that it should not be seen as the sole responsibility of schools or the education system. We caution against this because the tendency will be toward standardization and not to use measures that take account of Interests-Relationships-Practice and the other New Ways that lead to engaged learners. Furthermore, there will need to be a change in culture with Departments of Education not acting as regulators and creating unnecessary obstacles for these changes to take place.

Use Data to Drive Equity and Quality

Collecting data on work-based learning experiences is key to spotting trends, highlighting promising practices, and identifying and addressing gaps. Most states collect and disaggregate data on CTE programming to meet the data reporting expectations outlined in Perkins V. These data often include work-based learning opportunities, especially in states where work-based learning courses have unique course codes that enable states to collect participation data and disaggregate it by student demographics. However, many states offer work-based learning opportunities outside of CTE programming that are not measured in this CTE data reporting, meaning that CTE-based work-based learning data tell just a portion of the story. Just 20 states, including **Virginia, Tennessee, Iowa,** and **Maryland,** collect comprehensive data on work-based learning participation, including student outcomes.

POLICY RECOMMENDATION: It should be widely understood that what does not get measured cannot be improved. States must do better at collecting data on work-based learning and then using that data to drive equity and quality by setting up a means of collecting data on all work-based learning participants and the resulting outcomes.

All of our New Forms are externally evaluated on an ongoing basis so we can identify their strengths and improve our programs. As we have argued in Chapter Four on New Measures, we have to emphasize that how work-based learning and RWL are assessed is critical and needs to be reflected in policy and practice. If we rely solely on school-based measures that are standardized and designed only around school subjects, real student competencies will be missed and learning will be inhibited and teacher-led. We cannot measure New Ways and New Forms with Old Measures.Students need to be working to real-world standards, and employers have to contribute to and be involved in assessments related to that learning.

New Promising Policies and Practices

Several states have put in place or are proposing new and promising initiatives related to expanding and promoting work-based learning experiences. These include:

- **New York** is experimenting with new ways for students to earn a high school diploma. Some models in the state currently allow performance-based assessments, which could include student projects or other work, as an **alternative to Regents Exams.** State leaders are examining these models and plan to present recommendations to the Board of Regents in 2024 on how to change graduation requirements to include these alternative routes to a diploma.

- **Rhode Island** and **New Hampshire** are leading the way in **credit for learning** outside of the classroom. **New Hampshire** schools partner with others in their communities to offer Extended Learning Opportunities (ELO) to students after school hours, through experiences like internships, apprenticeships, community service, independent study and more. Student learning is measured by a school ELO team using competency-based assessments in line with state standards. **Rhode Island** has developed an All Course Network, a statewide course catalogue that lets students enrich their education

with learning in out-of-school time settings. Students can receive grades and high school elective credits for experiences like work-based learning and dual enrollment or advanced placement classes on another campus and build their own pathway to graduation. **Alabama, Mississippi, Montana, North Dakota, Arizona** and **West Virginia** have also enacted legislation that allow credit for learning that takes place beyond school hours[4].

- **Indiana** is considering a new bill that would establish **career scholarship accounts,** a voucher-like program that would provide funds to high school students to participate in apprenticeships or other job training. However, as of the time of this writing, many of the proposal details have not been finalized and questions remain around the program's cost, whether it would divert funding from traditional CTE, and whether students would have flexibility to change career pathways[5].

The Importance of Engaging Businesses

If educators and government comprise two legs of the work-based learning stool, business and employers are surely the third. Often, industry can play an outsized role in moving the needle on policy and be a powerful advocacy ally - once they understand the benefits.

Many of the policies outlined above are intended to remove the barrier that employers may have to participation or to incent their action. But first, employers must be persuaded that they have an equal part to play in ensuring that students have access to these programs. The lack of opportunity

4 Afterschool Alliance. 'Credit for Learning: Making Learning Outside of School Count,' http://afterschoolalliance.org/documents/issue_briefs/issue_credit_for_learning_79.pdf

5 Chalkbeat Indiana. https://in.chalkbeat.org/2023/1/18/23561558/indiana-high-school-graduation-diploma-career-technical-education-apprenticeship-scholarships-bill

for leaving to learn programs is not solely on schools to fix - employers must also agree that they should work with education leaders to create and expand quality programing.

There are many employers that are doing an excellent job of providing these opportunities. For example, for years **IBM** has led the way in ensuring their organization was not just benefiting from these skill-building programs but working with education and community leaders to build high-quality work-based learning programs that will ensure students have what they need to be successful. **Google** and **Microsoft** have created summer internship programs to boost the skills and social capital of students interested in STEM. And **Bank of America** and **John Hancock** have both created programs that support students interested in interning at non-profit organizations. These organizations are not just sitting on the sidelines and waiting for schools to solve a problem for them, but they are active participants in providing a solution for access to real-world learning. In order to provide a high-quality opportunity for every student, more employers must be willing to jump in the game and start providing these experiences.

It is important that the RWL opportunities offered by schools be comprehensive, covering all different types of occupations and careers. And of even greater importance is that employers are involved in what the students are learning. We offer this quote from the research: "When education-system actors have all the power, the result is school-based education or CTE that ignores the needs and opinions of employers. This leads to a number of common CTE program struggles, such as a mismatch between the education students received and the job market" (Renold et al. 2018, 4). Employers know real world standards in relation to

their business and profession. They need to be directly involved in this work and in the policies. They are an integral part of the community that is the school when the student is the curriculum.

Just Because You Build It, Doesn't Mean They'll Come: Changing Hearts and Minds

Ultimately, all the good policy in the world won't be enough to make leaving to learn the standard in education unless we get students and parents on board with the idea that these opportunities have value and can't be missed. Often, the biggest reason students and families shun a work-based learning experience at the high school level is a lack of course credit for the experience.

Some states, like **South Carolina,** have started to help districts build a course for non-CTE pathway students, centered around work-based learning, such as internship and apprenticeship, where the student can get course credit. Additionally, **South Carolina's** general assembly and legislators added work-based learning completion as a career ready qualifier to the state accountability system that affects high school report card ratings.

Perhaps the largest barrier to gaining student and parent acceptance, however, is just a simple lack of awareness. As cited previously, our studies show that only about a third of high school students know of any available work-based learning opportunities. Policymakers and practitioners must utilize all the tools at their disposal to spread the word, from traditional flyers, newsletters and email to videos, social media, blogs, websites and more. Some states make it a priority to designate certain days of the week for promotion; in **South Carolina,** for example, each Wednesday is 'Work-Based Learning

Wednesday,' a day set aside to highlight the various opportunities via social media, email blasts, websites, etc. Students have shown they want to learn and earn, when given the chance; if we build high-quality, accessible opportunities (and tell students about them), they will come.

We have learned that the best way to "spread the word" is by having students take the lead as ambassadors, promoters and demonstrators of the value of any program. We want to see students telling students about the amazing experiences they are having, sharing their interests and what they've learned, and how their RWL has made a difference in their lives. As Seymour Sarason says, "If you attempt to implement reforms but fail to engage the culture of a school, nothing will change".

Looking Ahead

The worldwide pandemic threatened to disrupt work-based learning on a wide scale, at a time when it's more important than ever to find ways to engage students in learning and ensure they are future ready. But educators, employers and students instead showed tremendous resilience, innovating virtual work-based learning experiences that, unconstrained by geographic proximity, actually expanded student access. Pioneering work-based learning programs took advantage of the pandemic as a learning opportunity and engaged students to develop solutions to real world problems. Many students made significant contributions at their workplace and had meaningful interactions with their employers, learning valuable remote work skills for the 21st-century workplace. Virtual work-based learning opportunities will no doubt continue to exist side-by-side with

in-person and hybrid offerings in the years ahead, and the policy infrastructure needs to be in place to support that evolution.

The Work-based Learning Alliance is one example of a pandemic policy initiative that has taken hold and has promise to expand opportunity. Originally started by the **Commonwealth of Massachusetts** as a means of creating high-quality virtual work-based learning experiences while students were out of school due to the pandemic, this initiative has recently become a stand-alone entity aimed at creating virtual experiences through state partnerships nationwide. With need far outpacing supply, states should look toward these high-quality virtual solutions as a promising practice.

Leaving to learn and work-based learning now stand on the precipice of an even larger period of expansion and growth. Educators struggling to re-engage students after the pandemic "lost" years are turning to career-connected education as a tool to energize and retain students through hands-on learning, showing them the connections between classroom and the real world. States should lean in on this and provide the resources necessary to see these programs thrive. Simultaneously, federal COVID relief funding provided to schools and states may be just the catalyst needed to spark robust investment in work-based learning as an education and workforce development tool. In fact, in late 2022, the US Department of Education released new guidance[6] that specifically suggests using this funding on expanding high-quality work-based learning and increasing opportunities for students to earn industry-sought credentials.

In 1987, my father, Kenneth Ryder, then president of Northeastern University, wrote the book *Cooperative Education in a New Era* (so you could say that a passion for work-

---

[6]   The U.S. Secretary of Education. http://ARP_Pathways_Dear_Colleague_11-14-22. 508

[7]   Ryder, K.G. and Wilson J.W. (1987) 'Cooperative Education in a New Era: Understanding and Strengthening the Link Between College and the Workplace', *Higher Education Policy* (1).

based learning is in my blood!). He wrote that cooperative education demonstrated its value in many ways: it is pedagogically sound; it is an effective and cost-efficient human resource strategy for employers; and it adapts to a variety of diverse institutional settings and fields of study. As he observed, "These are not only accomplishments of cooperative education, they constitute its fundamental strength as an educational method and will carry it, as such, into the future.'" Those words are as true today as they were then, and they certainly apply to not just cooperative education, but to all leaving to learn experiences. We are excited to see how out-of-school learning will continue to evolve and thrive in the 21st century and allow millions more students to connect real-world experiences to the classroom. However, the right policy infrastructure must be in place if we are to ensure there is a high-quality experience available to every student who would like to leave to learn.

Although Elliot never met Julie's dad, his first brush with Cooperative Education at Northeastern was in 1977 when one of his friends from Brooklyn was getting his Ph.D. in physiological psychology there. Vance was doing real work in the labs as he was putting his dissertation together. In those days there were many abandoned factories in the area around Northeastern and the university bought them up and had space that went out into the surrounding community. At that time, Elliot was at Harvard and pretty disillusioned there with classes that held little meaning, but when he went to visit Northeastern he was excited by the work and bantering there. It was great.

Over the course of decades, as Elliot and his colleagues worked to get students to leave to learn, he could not stop wondering about why we weren't doing this type of work in all

colleges, especially since Northeastern's job placement is around 93% across all of their disciplines. Compare that to other colleges and universities and you can easily see the influence of Cooperative Education. He also wondered about why schools in general were not getting more and more students and youth out earlier than college into the world and connected to adults around their interests to keep them engaged. The influence of his experiences at Northeastern certainly changed his way of practice as a teacher, principal, parent, and youth development director. Out of this and other influences came our schools and initiatives.

The next time Elliot came into contact with Northeastern was in the late '90's when BPL started a Principal Residency Program that developed new principals at our schools and in other schools around the country. An aspiring principal worked in their schools alongside principals who were top in their field. One of our partnering colleges for accreditation was Northeastern. This made perfect sense to everyone who was doing the principal residency work in Massachusetts. It was an easy fit and it produced a great cohort of principals.

*Of course, Julie never knew any of this and likewise, up until writing **Learning to Leave**, Elliot never knew who her father was at Northeastern. So, 50 years later the influence of something so profound as Cooperative Education comes together in this book and in our work. As Pam Roy, co-founder of B-Unbound, who just finished a book for parents on their role in getting children connected out in the real world, states: "Be a ripple in the water demonstrating how the power of community and self-organizing changes systems."*

🎙 TGIF

The school board of Newark approved a plan to have carpenters and a host of other employees who work for the school district have student interns. Does this mean that schools have now brought the outside inside? It is a very interesting policy that may resolve some issues around privacy and security of student data and allow far more students ways to connect to adults around their interests.

Yesterday, I was at the 311 Credential awards ceremony in Newark. There were around 50 people there honoring the 13 students who went through this ground-breaking program over the summer. Rob Smith, Executive Training Director at Eastern Atlantic States Carpenters Technical College, was present. He already set up a meeting for next week to take the 311 to other places in the Northeast and beyond. When the union gets behind an initiative, they can work wonders.

The "cast of thousands" continued with lots of politicians including Assemblyperson Eliana Pintor Marin, who gave a great talk. And then, the Executive Director of Newark Workforce Development Board, Karen Gaylord, who put the funds up for this work along with loads of big and small building contractors like Turner, Holt, McGinley, Interstate and Orion. As simple as it sounds, youth under 18 and without a GED or high school diploma were not allowed on site and could not enter into pre-apprenticeship programs. Now with the 311 they can. This is something that is hopefully going to spread. Everyone is bought in.

This is in large part because of what we knew all along about the combination of student interest and the adult-youth relationships around meaningful work. It is magical. Much thanks to Joe Youcha. He made it happen and to my compadre Charlie. If I ever experienced collective effervescence from a diverse group, this was it. And, the best part was that it was not a BPL event, it was everyones event.

On Tuesday at a meeting around internship development for all of Los Angeles. Andrea and I teamed up and had loads of practical advice to add to the discussion. From this meeting, it appears that initially, most of the internships will be afterschool and in the summer. Once again, state and district policies will have to change to get more students out during the school day. One such policy is to elevate internships to the status of AP classes.

Community Response

To go along with these lifestyle changes, earlier in the week, I started meeting with district people to implement BPLiving, the IBPLC and B-Unbound. Also, I was on a federal policy call about assessment. Honestly, being on this call was like being in the movie **Fifty First Dates**. The same people saying the same things promoting the same programs that have run up against the same opposition for the last 35 years. It was nice to catch up, but it appeared from the conversation that their message won't have much traction policy-wise, because there is nothing new here. How come this is the case? Well, if you don't change the Forms of school, you can't expect student assessment to change from where it is positioned. This is Reforms and New Measures, not New Forms and New Measures.

Pam's quote leads nicely on to the next point we want to make in this book about policy and RWL. For us, the New Ways, New Forms and New Measures are not just about a system response, but about a community response. We think that everybody needs to be in on this - of course, the education system, but we also need employers and workers, youth, their families, professionals, community leaders and everyone else who has a role in contributing to the learning of our young people. When all have some involvement, it's a community, and there is mutual responsibility - not pushing the blame or blaming one thing for wider or more collective mistakes. A community removes the siloes that feature in so much of our society.

Landscape with the Fall of Icarus
Pieter Bruegel the Elder, 1560

We think that Bruegel's painting, *Landscape with the Fall of Icarus,* reflects the lack of community connection in our present society and system. In the painting, Icarus has plummeted from near the sun into the sea and nobody appears to notice. All the adults are busy in their 'siloes'; no one is responsible, and nobody realizes that the boy will drown. How aware are we of the countless young people who are disengaged from school and are drowning in the system who need supportive adults and a community they can identify with? "In the USA in 2019, there were 2 million status dropouts between the ages of 16 and 24" (Note: this was before Covid). Status dropouts are 16- to 24-year-olds who are not enrolled in school and have not earned a high school credential (nces.ed.gov/fastfacts). Who is responsible? Is anyone seeking to prevent this from happening or are we just treating the symptoms once they get media attention?

From Interventions to Preventions

Our educational system is premised on the idea that everyone getting the same is desirable for learning and to create equity. If we give everybody the same technological equipment, the same test, the same standards and competencies, and the same instruction from a teacher, this seems like equality and fairness. Unfortunately, this produces a system that attempts to get at equity through standardized interventions rather than a system of personal prevention. An education system reliant on interventions has to focus excessive resources (people, time and money) in developing tests and over-testing students to see if they need to be part of an intervention program, and it remains mistakenly focused on standardizing narrow bands of content and delivery.

In comparison, a true prevention system that keeps bad things from happening would focus on the personal to understand the needs, wants and interests of students. Prevention would undermine and address the aspects within the system (the Deeper Four) that lead to student disengagement, dropout and poor mental health. Our education system, as with nearly any system, operates on the basis that people conform to it so that it can function efficiently towards its identified goals (i.e., graduation, improvement on test scores).

When the system experiences problems, like students dropping out, it tends to respond with intervention programs to "treat" students who are seen as most likely to drop out. This appears to make sense. You look at characteristics of youth who drop out, see what factors are strongly associated with dropping out, then try to identify younger students who have those traits and intervene to keep them on-track with remedial programs so they won't drop out when they get older. This seems like prevention. If I find that most high school dropouts have low reading ages and I provide extra reading support in elementary school for students who have scored low on English tests, then I'm trying to prevent these categories of young people dropping out.

The thing is, when the education system intervenes, it is really just treating and not preventing, and here's why. There are two big assumptions made that on the one hand, mix up cause and effect, and, on the other hand, make certain outcomes into problems which are not the real problems. To continue with our dropout example, what are the causes? The education system has always seen the causes as having to do with the students who drop out, NOT with what the school system does that may cause them to drop out. What happens is the traits of students who are seen as likely to drop out are taken as causes, so student factors (like their reading age, attendance or behavior) become the focus of intervention programs (to improve reading, attendance, behavior) which are intended to "prevent" them from dropping out. But it isn't clear or certain that these factors are causes; if they were, then any student who didn't attend school a certain number of times or who could only read at a certain level would drop out of school. The only thing we can say for definite is that some factors have a strong relationship to dropping out. The problem is that when we treat them as causes, then other factors, like those having to do with school, don't get considered or are never questioned.

The second assumption is that dropping out, for example, is a "problem", when we might see it instead as a predictable outcome or, in some instances, a good decision rather than a "problem". Usually, when something is seen as a problem, then there is a focus on solving it or making the situation better. Policies are built on problem solving, but what happens if we are addressing the wrong problems, or focusing on things that are not the causes, or the thing isn't a problem at all? The fact that we call it "dropping out" places the "blame" on the student. What if we called it "moving on" or "being pushed out" or "leaving to learn"?

We are not saying that dropping out of school is desirable or that it won't be a problem for a person who does (though in some cases it may be the best response to a bad situation). What we are saying is that when we make it the problem, we are overlooking all kinds of school factors, and we may be misled in thinking that certain student traits or variables are the cause of dropping out, and our policies and practices aimed at treating the "problem" with interventions may be misguided. The research evidence over the past 70 years shows that what

we have continued to do to "solve the problem of dropout" has not been working. So, do we just continue on with the same ways, conventional forms and old measures and ignore our friend Icarus?

Our attention is focused on school factors and that's why we believe in New Ways, New Forms and New Measures. It's not that we ignore important personal, cultural and socio-economic factors that children face but, from an educational policy perspective, we can do little to change them, AND we believe that there has been too much emphasis placed on interventions and trying to fix students rather than creating educational experiences that prevent disengagement and dropout. In a world filled with uncertainty and certainty, standards and variability, only humans can collectively think and feel in rhythm and time to dynamically respond to complex environmental stimuli, draw upon previous experience and intuitively understand what to do next. This is the work of educators, not algorithms.

We must consider a more varied set of competencies and also increase the ways that students can demonstrate that they have achieved them. Without the addition of many ways for students to achieve academic and real-world standards, we will only continue to incrementally develop an intervention system where ticking off pre-determined tasks is masked with words such as "mastery" and "personalization." But we should not be fooled. A true prevention system is based on an anywhere, anytime *and many ways* competency system.

TGIF

Intervention or prevention?

For policymakers, learning loss is the loss of time in a system that tries to keep students on track to graduate by a certain age, covering a certain amount of content and seeing how many get across the finish line given those parameters. Of course, all of this is a construct made up by people who themselves do well on tests and for some reason like to keep score with the caveat that all this is done for the greater good to everyone's economic benefit.

Once again, it could be me, but isn't loss about something or someone you had but lost? Isn't learning loss something you learned but lost? That we have plenty of. There's a ton we learn in and outside of school that got lost or forgotten, mostly from lack of use or utility. But, how can you lose something you never had in the first place? How do you get something you learned back if you never learned it?

COVID set the education system back on its heels. So, what are the system mavens to do? Intervene and put everyone in catch-up mode, pouring more money into going faster in less time, which is what they always wanted in the first place. Their primary methods of intervention here are 1:1 and small group tutoring, and online practice to get better scores on tests.

Pre-COVID New York State was already spending $25,000 per student. At that time the rates of proficiency on standardized tests were far from acceptable. Why didn't we institute tutoring on such a massive scale if, the evidence about tutoring was already there? Why are they spending all of this additional money now on afterschool,

summer school and extended day, teaching the same content taught during the school day? And why are they ignoring that if they looked more closely at the data, they would find that relationships between adult and child matter and that the teaching method matters for how a student learns? Sheeessh! Tutoring is more about relationships than they believe and not just about content and the method of delivery.

What can we do?

Pre-COVID Elliot wrote an article with Scott's help, "What Are We Losing by Keeping Students on Track?" Can students get credit for being off-track from the standard measures? Are schools adapting to the students or is it the other way around? Since this article, our New Forms and New Measures have added even more of a practical dimension to the possibilities of what can happen if we create more opportunities around prevention and not costly interventions.

In education, the policy is set for all students to graduate from college but only about 36% of adults have a college degree. How engaged are the majority of students when they are told school is only about going to college? And remember that just because you are going to college certainly doesn't mean you are engaged in school. Disengagement in school and community continues on into adult life with results that are very disheartening and troubling. If we are going to change the outcomes we want changed, we must engage our students and make them feel their lives have value and meaning for them in whatever productive paths they take. When outcomes look more like what you become, then we are moving in the right direction.

In this world where social media spreads in both productive and unproductive ways, how do we change the narrative around what it means to be smart? How do we get the public and policymakers to understand that certifications and diplomas without being attached to people and places in the real world is not enough? That what you know, and who knows you and knows you know, need to be connected and measured. Where does a campaign like this start? In a city? On social media? In schools? As policy? All of the above? These are challenges we will face when trying to spread our New Ways, New Forms and New Measures. We know we need research and data in our stories, and we know we are only part of the bigger picture if this is really going to change, but in this work our voices need to be heard and our practices need to influence.

Post-COVID is an opportune time to come back and be informed by evidence around: learning through interest and motivation and meaning; learning through practice in real-world learning environments; and learning through relationships both in and outside of school (i.e., advisory and place-based learning experiences). It is a time to be informed by health and lifestyle medicine evidence that impacts learning across the board for the general society but especially in the most marginalized communities, where the health disparities are far greater due to racism and food industry marketing.

What Will Change Schools?

For all the hard work, endless time and money spent on school reform, little has changed in public education. Most schools are still going about business in the same way with some slight variations on a theme. If you were on the moon, what goes on in education on Earth all looks about the same as it always did for the last 70 years. This raises questions about how to change large systems. As Peter Senge, the MIT professor and author of the *Fifth Discipline: The Art and Practice of the Learning Organization* (1990) reminds us, the first principle of systems theory is: "The harder you push, the harder the system pushes back. This is the response of a system trying to survive" (43). Senge adds: "The cure lies with the relationships with the very people we typically blame for the problems we are trying to solve" (52).

Systems resist change, but sometimes there are ways that a system is changed because an innovation is so powerful and gets to the public so fast that the system is forced to adjust and move into the change rather than pushing on the innovation and nullifying it. The innovation can enter the system from the edge and change the center. Most strategies for changing public education have gone the route of making ideas into policy through the system. This is no surprise since almost the entire school system is set up to deliver learning from concept to practice - and that's being kind. Many a "sound step" has been pushed aside by the school system. Like the example in Chapter Four of getting on the floor and dancing in *Strictly Ballroom,* there are possibilities where public education can also be changed in more immediate ways by getting actions and ideas out far enough into communities so that they change the system rather than the system changing them.

The example of the Napster phenomenon may hold some keys to making a system change around the strengths of an innovation that is more immediate and direct. Established in 1999, Napster only lasted 2 years but it led to systemic change in the music industry because it got to the public coming from the edge. Napster was an internet file sharing application that allowed users to share their music files (MP3s) with each other. If you had Napster it was easy to download copies of songs and then pass them on to your friends. It is estimated that there were up to about 80 million Napster users, and it paved the way for streaming media services.

The music industry, the status quo, was shaken up by Napster and it resisted. Eventually, it seems lawsuits about copyright infringements and violations ended Napster in 2001, but the music business had no alternative but to change. It was hard for the industry to control where it was going because things gathered momentum in a very public way, and it was what the public wanted. This use then changed the system rather than waiting for the system to create a policy that mandates the use.

It is interesting to look at how Napster might be a way to change schools, because the music industry regulation of file sharing and streaming and its draw back into the music business has permanently changed the system. Is it possible that something like a Napster will come along in education? Will such a disruption allow the public to have choice and lead to changes in the education system from state bureaucracies, local school districts, colleges and universities, and book publishing companies? Can RWL have a similar disruption to education that will do what Napster did to the music industry?

A large segment of the regressive thinking of the standardization (not standards) movement takes us back to the factory age where the mentality was to standardize everything including education. This model has been alive and well in schools and has produced, by its own assessment, poor results on issues of equity for all children; however, we have now entered an age where learning is personal, where you can educate yourself or get educated about what you are interested in bypassing the conventional routes. Most people have access to do this through learning sources and resources without having to enter a school. Starting in the 1950's, television brought us more information, but the internet brings us any information we want when we want it. The delivery of information, like the delivery of music through a Napster or Spotify-like platform, can lead us to new breakthroughs in the system.

You might think that the growth of home schooling coupled with a delivery system of where to get what you want may change the system, but it has not because home schooling broadly operates with the same ways, forms and measures of the system. This is akin to the growth of online learning during COVID that brought the same content and instructional delivery into homes, only the medium changed but not the method. Form followed the old function, so no New Measures were required and no New Ways and New Forms took shape. The Napster effect was caused by getting far enough out there in the community to make the decision but then resonating with the center so that the rest of the system needed to change itself. New Ways, New Forms and New Measures ignore the system for the sake of learning and equity - will they be discovered by the center?

 TGIF

If you come from a long line of pool players like me, you have probably heard of a technique called edge to center. In order to make a cut shot, you line up the edge of the cue ball with the edge of the ball you are going to hit. Then, you move your cue

stick to the center of the cue ball, et viola! The ball goes in the pocket. This edge to the center shot is a good metaphor. Line up what students are doing at their edge and then, aim for the center.

What these two edge-to-the-center examples point to is that there are many ways to get to the center. In both cases, to get there you start at the edges. And, although we talk about giving credit for student work anywhere, anytime, it is debatable (or highly unlikely) whether this really has changed or will change anything around equity by starting at the center. This is because these changes are about maintaining an assessment system of winners and losers. Unless we credit the many ways that students can demonstrate competency, there is still only one way. Starting from the edge gets schools to understand the many ways that students can show competence and will produce more equitable ways students can show they are smart.

If we want to get our students to the center and stay learner centered, I suggest we start where they are meaningfully learning outside of school at the edges inventing, discovering, creating, understanding. They go there to keep themselves in balance and find their center. They go there because this is where they are learning, at the edge of their competence. It is there and then, our work as adults is to be with, guide, manage, facilitate, enrich and instruct.

Finally, a word of caution. Remember when the edge becomes the center, we start Centers for the Edge and, in doing so, we lose our edge. Although formal policy statements are significant ways to produce certainty, we should not overlook how the culture and regularities of schools and schooling build into calcified systems and structures.

 Micah

My name is Micah, I'm a 12th grader in Santa Monica and I like to write. Specifically, I like to write movies and television shows - scripts. This passion for writing has persisted all throughout high school. I have done all I can to improve my craft by learning screenwriting software, reading books and watching movies, and meeting with a mentor, Robert Morgan Fisher, who is an award-winning short story writer, talented songwriter, professional screenwriter, and writing professor at UCLA Extension and Antioch University.

I started meeting with Robert as my mentor three years ago. I have spent one school day a week with him most of the three years. Even when I lived in another country for a semester in 11th grade, Robert and I met on Zoom and emailed about my writing. Robert taught me how to write scripts. He showed me how when we were together, encouraged me to keep writing on my own, and helped me improve my work in the next session. He recommends books, movies, and shows for me. Per his recommendation, I've watched everything from guides designed to teach the fundamentals of screenwriting to comedy shows and movies he thinks I'll get a kick out of.

Living in Southern California, I'm surrounded by people with immigration stories. My own family were immigrants who fled violence in Russia generations ago. I wanted to write an immigration story. Robert and I began brainstorming. I first came up with a loose plot outline, then created the protagonist, antagonist, and guiding character (the central three characters of any story). The more Robert and I discussed it, the clearer the story became.

During our discussions I wrote a bullet pointed list of scenes and plot points. That list eventually became a slugline script: a list of scene headings and brief descriptions of what happens in each scene. I think of it as the skeleton of a script. From there, it was just a matter of filling it in; I wrote properly formatted action and dialogue in place of paragraphs of scene descriptions. Each week I would write a couple of scenes on my own, then Robert would go over it and suggest improvements. Then I would make improvements and write some more. This process went on for a year and a half. As I went along, Robert and I talked through new ideas to implement into the script. By the time it was finished, the script looked wildly different from the original slugline script.

At this point, Robert encouraged me to hold a table reading of the script. Together we gathered a cast of talented, working actors to read the words I wrote. Robert is now aiding me in getting my script in front of agents and industry executives. In addition to all of this, he also listened and gave feedback on my college essays. He is a mentor, a friend, and along with my family, he is my biggest supporter. He is the reason I am the writer I am today.

*While I have honed my writing skills with Robert, I have also been learning about the business side of the industry through my internship at Lionsgate Entertainment. In 9th grade, I had a shadow day there. I sat in on a finance meeting, only understanding a third of what was discussed. I was given a script to read, which has now been made into a movie. I got a tour of the building. There were displays and posters from famous movies like The **Twilight** and **Hunger Games** trilogies. Eventually, the shadow day became an internship. I spend one day a week at Lionsgate doing script coverage, reviewing*

scripts and passing my feedback up the line, doing research, budgeting and inputting information into Excel spreadsheets, and sometimes sitting in on meetings. It's incredibly cool to be there and very informative. I'm welcomed in the office and trusted with important tasks. I feel as though I understand the business side of the film and TV industry now.

Student-Driven Learning Plans

Our system needs to transform from reform into New Forms and get creative about effectively serving each and every one of our students without excuses. The development and system-wide implementation of learning plans would be a powerful way to help educators think about how they would reorganize the way they use time, people, and other resources available for learning in a system of prevention with anywhere, anytime, anyway competencies. We have seen the ways in which these approaches can truly transform student learning (we just met Micah), and feel that the widespread adoption of these changes from interventions to prevention would have a substantial impact on the transformation of schools to better prepare students for their futures. What are we waiting for?

A system that is based on prevention truly puts each and every student at the center by uncovering their interests and needs and establishing opportunities in and outside of school to follow through with a longitudinal plan. If students are truly at the center of their learning, then they are given real choices about what they learn. A learning plan for every student is both pegged to high standards and also sees each student as an individual honoring who they are.

The use of student learning plans puts the focus on learning by cultivating the conditions that enhance learning. It values and promotes learning opportunities that are challenging, that address real-world standards, and that augment social emotional learning. The use of learning plans elucidates the fact that the learning process is a complex mixture of many things including motivations, intelligences, personalities and relationships.

A student-driven learning plan is a tool to bring together students, parents, teachers, and others who might serve as educators to design a flexible, long-range learning plan with very specific immediate and short-term learning goals. The learning plan is based on learning goals that reflect high standards and value each child's specific interests and strengths. It provides specifics about what a student will learn and the kinds of learning activities that may be appropriate for that learning. The plan evolves with the student and incorporates all of the work that she does in school as well as the outside of school learning experiences that she engages in, such as internships and volunteer service. The learning plan assures that relevant, authentic contexts are established for learning for each student and that that learning is aligned to authentic standards drawn from the workplace and the community as well as the school that matter to all. This produces true student grit and resiliency displayed both in and outside of school, in homes and communities. With the support of the community, students simultaneously grow socially and emotionally.

The benefits of student at the center learning plans are that they bring substantial focus to the learning for students as well as for their family. Plans allow everyone to focus on the whole child, including together their physical, emotional and mental health, not just on what the child is learning in a particular subject or on a particular strength or weakness. In this era of accountability, the learning plan is the ultimate accountability tool, enabling students, parents, teachers, and mentors to be "account-able" for learning over time that starts with preventions rather than interventions and uses technology to develop, document, archive, support, and manage the plan over time.

The final piece we want to share in this book was written by Kapua Chandler who is leading the establishment of the Namahana School with a BPL partnership in Hawaii. Her reflection captures what it means to have community engagement and responsibility where the learner is the curriculum and the land and the people are the school, an environment where new ways of knowing emerge.

Namahana's School design is developed from the values and educational needs of the Koʻolau and Haleleʻa communities on the island of Kauaʻi. Namahana School plans to utilize ʻĀina-based learning (ʻĀBL) throughout the school model. ʻĀina meaning that which feeds us - physically, spiritually, emotionally, intellectually and in all ways - most often in reference to lands, rivers, streams, and oceans. ʻĀBL is a dynamic approach to education in which learners can deepen their relationship with the land and its resources, cultivate connections within their communities, and build critical skills that can be applied to real-world issues and meet the needs of the whole community from keiki to kupuna (child to elder).

This experience-based learning style and knowledge sharing offers students the opportunity to engage in holistic, community-driven solutions that can address 21st century social, economic, and environmental challenges. ʻĀBL will help to

At Namahana School, we firmly believe that in order to take care of a community (people and place) you must develop and maintain a relationship to that place. 'ĀBL is a structured way to provide opportunities to develop deep relationships with their community lands, waters, oceans, and people. It is through the development of these relationships that students will grow a sense of kuleana (responsibility) to care for their place. Similar to the ways a grandchild cares for their grandparent, we see 'āina as a living entity that we must get to know in order to mālama (care for) our place in a pono (proper, balanced) way. From mo'olelo (stories), mele (songs), oli (chants) and hula (dance) to observations, data collection, to policy and action, 'ĀBL provides an opportunity to build a relationship with place in order to better understand how to protect and steward our natural resources and ourselves.

instill a sense of kuleana (responsibility) to mālama (care for) place, people, and planet with the flexibility to tailor learning plans to the interests and goals of each student.

Namahana School is unique in that it prioritizes connections with the 'āina and community; the 'ĀBL model will be deeply grounded in real-life experiences with and on the 'āina (land, water, oceans), in the very places many of our students and families have lived for generations. Namahana students will gain knowledge and skills from community organizations, kupuna (elders), local businesses, and other local leaders through field studies and internships. Students will also have opportunities to explore their interests, and work on addressing issues that directly affect the communities in which they live. Our 'ĀBL model and assessment practices differ from other place-based models in that students' learning must maintain and mālama (care for) relationships in the community.

Kapua's description of Namahana is a fitting way to bring our book to a close. We hope we have stimulated some interest, challenged some perceptions, shaken a few assumptions, and provoked you to take action. We believe that policy has to be guided by practice, that form should follow function, and that we must no longer pursue or be content with RE-FORM. We feel that our New Ways, New Forms and New Measures open the path for transforming education.

We realize that there are many people out there in communities and in schools who are doing work that connects with our New Ways, New Forms and New Measures. We want to hear from you, and we want to encourage you in your efforts.

We are energized by the last 10 years, and we will continue to mingle with and muddle through these things that matter to young people and that help them find meaning in their lives. Yes, they are our future BUT they are their present, and we want to continue to value that, recognize their interests, foster and facilitate opportunity-opening relationships, and allow every young person who wants to practice in the real world the chance to do so. We are hopeful but we are not idealists, we are pragmatists, not theorists but practitioners. We wanted to share our learning in the expectation that you will challenge us to learn more, to do better, to fine tune and find even more New Ways, New Forms and New Measures to transform education.

Avanti...

Bibliography

Afterschool Alliance. 'Credit for Learning: Making Learning Outside of School Count,' http://afterschoolalliance.org/documents/issue_briefs/issue_credit_for_learning_79.pdf

American Student Assistance and Bellwether Education Partners. (March, 2021) 'Working to Learn and Learning to Work A state-by-state analysis of high school work-based learning policies.' https://file.asa.org/uploads/ASA-Bellwether-WBL-Policies.pdf

American Student Assistance. (March 2022) 'High School Work-based Learning: Best Practices Designed to Improve Career Readiness Outcomes for Today's Youth.' https://asa.org/wp-content/uploads/2023/01/ASA_WBLPlaybook_Final.pdf

American Student Assistance. 'Best Practices in Youth Work-based Learning: Ensure Broad Eligibility and Widespread Equitable Access'. https://www.asa.org/research/best-practices-in-youth-work-based-learning-ensure-broad-eligibility-and-widespread-equitable-access

Bloom, D. B. (ed.) (1985) *Developing Talent In Young People*. New York: Ballantine Books.

Blustein, D. L. (2011) 'A relational theory of working.' *Journal of Vocational Behavior*. Netherlands: Elsevier Science, 79, 1-17.

Boldt, S. (1998) *Showing the Way: Responses and approaches to the needs of students and early school leavers*. Dublin: Marino Institute of Education.

Boldt, S. (2004) *Alternative Education for Under 15's: International Perspectives*. Dublin: Marino Institute of Education.

Boyer, E. (1995) 'The Educated Person,' *The 1995 ASCD Yearbook*. The Association for Supervision and Curriculum Development.

Bruner, J. (1990) *Acts of meaning*. Cambridge, MA, US: Harvard University Press (Acts of meaning).

Brunner, E., Dougherty, S. and Ross, S. (2019) 'The Effects of Career and Technical Education,' August 2019 http://www.edworkingpapers.com/ai19-112

Caillois, R. (1958) *Les jeux et les hommes: le masque et le vertige*. Paris: Gallimard.

Callahan, J., Ito, M., Rea, S. C. and Wortman, A. (2019) *Influences on Occupational Identity in Adolescence: A Review of Research and Programs.* Irvine, CA: Connected Learning Alliance.

Camera, L. (2016) "Achievement Gap Between White and Black Students Still Gaping" US NEWS and World Report. https://www.usnews.com/news/blogs/data-mine/2016/01/13/achievement-gap-between-white-and-black-students-still-gaping

Chalkbeat Indiana. https://in.chalkbeat.org/2023/1/18/23561558/indiana-high-school-graduation-diploma-career-technical-education-apprenticeship-scholarships-bill

Chalkiadaki, A. (2018) 'A Systematic Literature Review of 21st Century Skills and Competencies in Primary Education.' *International Journal of Instruction,* 11 (3), 1-16.

Childress, H. (2000) *Landscapes of Betrayal, Landscapes of Joy: Curtisville in the Lives of Its Teenagers.* Illustrated edition, Albany: State University of New York Press.

Consumer News and Business Channel (CNBC). 'Fewer kids are going to college because they say it costs too much.' https://www.cnbc.com/2021/03/14/fewer-kids-going-to-college-because-of-cost.html

Crawford, C. (1984) *The Art of Computer Game Design.* USA: McGraw-Hill, Inc.

Cremin, L. A. (1976) *Public Education.* Basic Books.

Csikszentmihalyi, M. and Schneider, B. (2001) *Becoming Adult: How Teenagers Prepare for the World of Work.* New York: Perseus Books.

Educational Credit Management Corporation (ECMC) - Question the Quo. 'Gen Z Teens Want Shorter, More Affordable, Career-Connected Education Pathways.' https://www.questionthequo.org/media/3954/qtq-survey-5-digital-report.pdf

Deci, E. L. and Ryan, R. M. (2008) 'Self-determination theory: A macrotheory of human motivation, development, and health.' *Canadian Psychology / Psychologie Canadienne.* US: Educational Publishing Foundation, 49, 182-185.

Fisher, J. F. (2018) *Who You Know: Unlocking Innovations That Expand Students' Networks.* 1st edition, San Francisco, CA: Jossey-Bass.

Frankl, V. (1959) *Man's Search for Meaning.* New York: Random House.

Gray, L. and Lewis, L. (2018) *Career and Technical Education Programs in Public School Districts: 2016–17: First Look.* US Department of Education: National Centre for Education Statistics.

Grohl, V. H. (2018) *From Cradle to Stage: Stories from the Mothers Who Rocked and Raised Rock Stars.* London: Coronet Publishing..

Hagger, M.S. and Chatzisarantis, N. (2016) 'The Trans-Contextual Model of Autonomous Motivation in Education: Conceptual and Empirical Issues and Meta-Analysis,' *Review of Educational Research* 86 (2).

Hendren, S. (2020) *What Can a Body Do?: How We Meet the Built World.* Illustrated edition, New York: Riverhead.

Ingold, T. (2017) 'Knowing from the Inside: Anthropology, Art, Architecture and Design,' Aberdeen: European Research Council (ERC) and the University of Aberdeen.

Ingold, T. ed. (2022) Knowing from the Inside: Cross-Disciplinary Experiments with Matters of Pedagogy. London: Bloomsbury Academic.

Jacobs, J. (1993). The death and life of great American cities. Vintage Books.

Johnston, J. and Milligan, S. (2020) *The Design and Validation of the International Big Picture Learning Credential (IBPLC),* Assessment Research Centre, University of Melbourne.

Jukes, M. C. H., Sitabkhan, Y., and Tibenda, J. J. (2021). *Adapting Pedagogy to Cultural Context. RTI Press.* https://doi.org/10.3768/rtipress.2021.op.0070.2109

Kenny, M. E. (2013) 'The promise of work as a component of educational reform.' *In The Oxford handbook of the psychology of working.* New York, NY, US: Oxford University Press (Oxford library of psychology), 273-291.

Kohn, A. (2004) *What Does It Mean to Be Well Educated?: And More Essays on Standards, Grading, and Other Follies: 0.* Boston, Mass: Beacon Press.

Kohn, A. (2015) 'Progressive Education: Why it's Hard to Beat, But Also Hard to Find.' *Progressive Education in Context.*

Koven, B. D. (2013) *The Well-Played Game: A Player's Philosophy.* Illustrated edition, Cambridge, Massachusetts: MIT Press.

Lave, J. and Wenger, E. (1991) *Situated learning: Legitimate peripheral participation.* New York, NY, US: Cambridge University Press.

Marsalis, W. and Ward, G.C. (2008) *Moving to Higher Ground: How Jazz Can Change Your Life.* New York: Random House.

Milligan, S., Luo, R., Kamei, T., Rice, S. and Kheang, T. (2020) *Recognition of learning success for all.* Melbourne, Victoria: Learning Creates Australia.

Milligan, S. K., Luo, R., Hassim, E., and Johnston, J. (2020). *Future-proofing students: What they need to know and how to assess and credential them.* Melbourne, Australia: Melbourne Graduate School of Education, the University of Melbourne: Melbourne.

Milligan, S., Hassim, E., Rice, S., and Kheang, T. (2021) Generating trust and utility in senior secondary certification: Case studies of first movers in their warranting networks. Melbourne: Learning Creates Australia.

National Health and Nutrition Examination Survey Questionnaire (NHANES). (2021) "Adult Obesity Statistics." Hyattsville, MD: U.S. Department of Health and Human Services, Centers for Disease Control and Prevention. www.cdc.gov/obesity/data/adult.html

OECD (2006), *Think Scenarios, Rethink Education,* Schooling for Tomorrow series, Paris: OECD.

OECD (2015) 'Skills Beyond School: Synthesis Report,' *Reviews of Vocational Education and Training.* Geneva: OECD.

Philips, K. and Jenkins, A. (2018) 'Communicating Personalized Learning to Families and Stakeholders: Terminology, Tools and Tips for Success,' ExcelinEd and Education Elements.

Podmore, B., Fonagy, P. and Munk, S. (2016) *Characterizing Mentoring Programs for Promoting Children and Young People's Wellbeing.* London: University College.

Popham, W.J. (1998) *Classroom Assessment: What Teachers Need to Know.* 2nd ed, Boston: Allyn and Bacon.

Popham, W.J. (2002) *What Every Teacher Should Know About Educational Assessment.* London: Pearson.

PR Newswire. 'Big Picture Learning and American Student Assistance Partner to Provide Internship Opportunities to Thousands of Students Across the State of California.' https://www.prnewswire.com/news-releases/big-picture-learning-and-american-student-assistance-partner-to-provide-internship-opportunities-to-thousands-of-students-across-the-state-of-california-301364603.html

Renold, U., Bolli, T., Caves, K., Bürgi, J., Egg, M.E., Kemper, J. and Rageth, L. (2018) *Comparing International Vocational Education and Training Programs.* Zurich: The National Center on Education and the Economy.

Robert, M. (2018) 'How to Address the Marine Skills' Shortage.' https://blog.v-hr.com/blog/how-to-address-the-marine-skills-shortage

Robinson, K. (2009) *The Element: How Finding Your Passion Changes Everything.* London: Penguin.

Robinson, K. (2015) *Creative Schools: Revolutionizing Education from the Ground Up.* London: Allen Lane.

Ryder, K. G. and Wilson, J. W. (1987) *Cooperative Education in a New Era: Understanding and Strengthening the Links between College and the Workplace.* Jossey-Bass Publishers, 433 California Street, San Francisco, CA 94104.

Ryder, K.G. and Wilson J.W. (1987) 'Cooperative Education in a New Era: Understanding and Strengthening the Link Between College and the Workplace', *Higher Education Policy* (1).

Salisbury, A.D. and Kraft, K. (2020) *Unlocking Career Potential: An Analysis of the Career Navigation & Guidance Product Landscape.* San Francisco: Entangled Solutions.

Sarason, S. (1990) *The Predictable Failure of Educational Reform: Can We Change Course Before It's Too Late?* San Francisco: Jossey-Bass.

Sarason, S. (2004) *And What Do You Mean By Learning?* New Hampshire: Heinemann.

Schweisfurth, M. (2020) *Future Pedagogies: Reconciling Multifaceted Realities and Shared Vision.* UNESCO.

Scott, C. (2015) 'The Futures of Learning 2: What Kind of Learning for the 21st Century?' UNESCO.

Senge, P. M. (1990) *The Fifth Discipline: The Art and Practice of the Learning Organization.* New York: Doubleday.

Soricone, L. (2020) *Breaking Ground: A First Look at American High School Skilled Trades Education. Jobs for the Future.* Jobs for the Future.

Sosniak, L. A. (1989) *Partnerships with a purpose: a case study on curriculum development and delivery through school-college collaboration.* New York: College Entrance Examination Board.

Stewart, S. and Haynes, C. (2016) 'An Alternative Approach to Standardized Testing: A Model That Promotes Racial Equity and College Access.' *Journal of Critical Scholarship on Higher Education and Student Affairs,* 2 (1).

Sullivan, L. (1896) 'The Tall Office Building Artistically Considered.' *Lippincott's Monthly Magazine.*

The U.S. Secretary of Education. http://ARP_Pathways _Dear_Colleague_11-14-22. 508

UNESCO (2021) *Reimagining our futures together: a new social contract for education.* UNESCO.

Van Dam, A. 'The happiest, least stressful, most meaningful jobs in America,' *The Washington Post,* January 6, 2023.

Viennet, R. and Pont, B. (2017) 'Education Policy Implementation: A Literature Review and Proposed Framework,' *OECD Education Working Paper No. 162.* Paris: OECD.

Voogt, J. and Roblin, N. P. (2010) *21st Century Skills.* Enschede: University of Twente.

Voogt, J. and Roblin, N. P. (2012) 'A comparative analysis of international frameworks for 21st century competences: Implications for national curriculum policies.' *Journal of Curriculum Studies.* Routledge, 44 (3), 299-321.

Vygotsky, L. (1986) *The Mind and Society.* Boston: MIT Press.

Waldinger, R. and Schulz, M. (2023) *The Good Life: Lessons from the World's Longest Study on Happiness.* London: Rider.

Washor, E. and Mojkowski, C. (2013) *Leaving to Learn: How Out-of-school Learning Increases Student Engagement and Reduces Dropout Rates.* Heinemann.

Wenger, E. (1998) *Communities of practice: Learning, meaning, and identity.* New York, NY, US: Cambridge University Press.

Wilson, F. R. (1998) *The Hand: How Its Use Shapes the Brain, Language, and Human Culture.* New York: Pantheon Books.

Yunkaporta, T. (2019) *Sand Talk: How Indigenous Thinking Can Save the World.* Melbourne, Victoria: The Text Publishing Company.

About the Authors

You can follow the authors' ongoing work on **www.bigpicturelearning.org** or you can email Elliot at **ewashor@gmail.com** or Scott at **sdavidboldt@gmail.com**

Elliot Washor

Elliot Washor has always held that the key to education - and really to humanity - is to have students and staff - and people in general - mingle with and muddle through problems that matter to them and their communities. If this seems simple, it's intended to. As co-founder of Big Picture Learning and The Metropolitan Regional Career and Technical Center, Elliot's educational philosophy - one which is embedded at the core of Big Picture's successful school design - is that practice should inform theory and that theory should inform practice, a cycle that can lead to profound change, and one that has earned Elliot wide acclaim and recognition.

Elliot was selected as one of the Twelve Most Daring Educators in the world by the George Lucas Educational Foundation. He has won a Ford Award in State and Local Government. His dissertation, 'Innovative Pedagogy and New Facilities' won the merit award from DesignShare, the international forum for innovative schools. Elliot has won a regional Emmy for his work as an Executive Producer on Big Picture Learning's early Public Service Announcements and recently his short film, *Navigating Our Way*, was awarded best animation in the Boston International Film Festival.

Elliot lives in sunny San Diego with his wife and dogs.

Scott Boldt

S cott Boldt agrees with what one of his mentors, Ray Houghton, used to say, "The goal of education should be to help people to learn to live with ambiguity." Scott, originally from Chicago, has lived more than half his life on the island of Ireland. His early career in education involved 'practice informing theory' as he wrote a dozen books and more articles focused on addressing the needs of young people who leave school early. His work has been translated into Dutch, French and Korean and he served as National Director for Ireland to the European Observatory on Innovation in Education and Training.

After marrying and migrating from Dublin to Belfast, Scott was involved in the peace process in Northern Ireland, directing the Peace and Reconciliation Program at Queen's University which led to subsequent work in the Balkans. He serves as Research Associate at Leeds-Beckett University and Professor of Practice at the National University of Wales, Trinity-St. David and at the University of Cumbria. He co-wrote the short film, *HORN OK PLEASE*, which won Best Animation Film at the Irish Film and Television Awards.

Scott lives in not-so-sunny Belfast with his family, dogs, cats, hen and ten year-old goldfish.